THE GREAT PRAYER

To
Walter Gervase Bennett

THE
GREAT
PRAYER

Concerning the Canon
Of the Mass

Hugh Ross Williamson

GRACEWING

First published in 1955 by Collins,
this edition published 2009

Gracewing
2 Southern Avenue, Leominster
Herefordshire, HR6 0QF

The right of Hugh Ross Williamson to be identified as the author of this work has been asserted in accordance with the Copyright, Designs and Patents Act 1988.

Cover design by Reynolds Stone

ISBN 978 0 85244 295 1

PREFACE TO THE SECOND EDITION

During the last century, a movement arose of opposition to the Roman Canon. Comparative study had revealed how different the "Roman" Eucharist Prayer is from those used in other rites of early origin and had convinced some liturgical scholars that it had hardly deserved to be classified as a Eucharistic prayer at all. Consequently, when the Mass was being reformed after the Second Vatican Council, there were those who argued that the Roman Canon should be radically revised or even abandoned altogether.

However, in the Roman Missal promulgated in 1970, Pope Paul VI decided that the Roman Canon, a prayer that has been in constant use among God's people for over fifteen hundred years, should be retained almost unchanged and be placed as the first amongst the three other Eucharistic prayers of more recent composition. The Roman Canon suffered in these new surroundings by comparison with its companions. It is longer and its style more complex.

Despite the fact that the Roman Canon may not have been amongst the most popular in usage in recent years Hugh Ross Williamson's study of *The Great Prayer* shows what great treasures are to be uncovered in this anaphora.

Brought up as a Congregationalist, the author was in Anglican orders when he wrote this book. Soon afterwards, he sought full communion with the Church of Rome. He moves slowly through the prayer to shed light on every detail, and includes some astute theological, spiritual and liturgical reflections. While this is not the most up-to-date scholarly work on this Eucharistic Prayer, it does nevertheless hold its value. Its freshness of style will make it a pleasant as well as an informative read for today.

I commend this book to all who wish to discover afresh the riches of the Church's Liturgy and thus to renew her life.

✠ **Alan S Hopes**
Titular Bishop of Chester le Street
Auxiliary Bishop of Westminster

CONTENTS

CONTENTS

CONTENTS

INTRODUCTION

WHETHER OR NOT Jesus Christ was born of woman, lived, suffered, died, was buried and rose from the dead to ascend in glory to Heaven cannot be established by ordinary historical evidence. The only witness is in the traditions and writings of the Church.

The story of Christ rests entirely on the word of His early followers. The New Testament, (which was not finally authenticated by the Church till three hundred years later,) supplements and in part embodies the traditional teaching of the Church. And in the New Testament we can read how Christ consistently refused to give the kind of 'sign' which would have found its way into ordinary history. When tempted to perform a miracle by throwing Himself down from the Temple when Jerusalem was crowded with visitors from all over the world, He refused to do it. When He was on the cross and Jerusalem had come out to see Him die, He was challenged again: "Come down from the Cross and we will believe." It would indeed have been *stupor mundi*, but again He refused. When He rose from the dead, He did not show Himself to Pilate or to Caiaphas or to the crowds who had watched him die. He showed Himself, as Peter admitted: "Not to all the people, but to us . . ."

Because Christianity is an historical religion, based on events in time and place, it is assumed too often, even by Christians, that those events are as historically verifiable as, for instance, the career of Napoleon is historically verifiable. Because we can point to classical references to a sect which *believed* in Christ, many jump to the untenable conclusion that that belief is objective evidence of the facts they wish to establish. But history comes in later and in a different way.

What is inescapable for the most sceptical historian is not the fact of the Incarnate Body of Christ, but the fact of his Mystical Body, the Church. Whether or not on a particular Thursday evening in an upper room in Jerusalem, Jesus of Nazareth ordered His followers till the end of time to eat his Body and drink his Blood under the species of bread and wine can never be 'historically' established. But that for nineteen centuries this has been done cannot be 'historically' escaped.

Dom Gregory Dix put the matter thus in a great passage in *The Shape of the Liturgy*: "Was ever another command so obeyed? For century after century, spreading slowly to every continent and country and among every race on earth, this action has been done, in every conceivable human circumstance, for every conceivable human need from infancy, and before it to extreme old age and after it, from the pinnacles of earthly greatness to the refuge of fugitives in the caves and dens of the earth. Men have found no better thing than this to do for kings at their crowning and for criminals going to the scaffold; for armies in triumph or for a bride and bridegroom in a little country church; for the proclamation of a dogma or for a good crop of wheat; for the wisdom of a

Parliament of a mighty nation or for a sick old woman afraid
to die; for a schoolboy sitting an examination or for Columbus
setting out to discover America; for the famine of whole
provinces or for the soul of a dead lover; in thankfulness
because my father did not die of pneumonia; for a village
headman much tempted to return to fetich because the yams
had failed; because the Turk was at the gates of Vienna; for
the repentance of Margaret; for the settlement of a strike;
for a son for a barren woman; for Captain So-and-So,
wounded and prisoner of war; while the lions roared in the
nearby amphitheatre; on the beach at Dunkirk; while the
hiss of scythes in the thick June grass came faintly through the
windows of the church; tremulously by an old monk on the
fiftieth anniversary of his vows; furtively, by an exiled bishop
who had hewn timber all day in a prison camp near Mur-
mansk; gorgeously, for the canonisation of St. Joan of Arc
—one could fill many pages with reasons why men have done
this and not tell a hundredth part of them. And best of all,
week by week and month by month, on a hundred thousand
successive Sundays, faithfully, unfailingly, across all the
parishes of Christendom, the pastors have done this just to
make the plebs sancta Dei—the holy, common people of
God." ⌋

The unique phenomenon in history is the *Church*—that is
to say, the company of people which no man now can number
who eat, have eaten and will eat the Body, who drink, have
drunk and will drink the Blood.

ˊ This company is by no means the same as the well-
intentioned many who give general assent to the principles
enunciated in the 'Sermon on the Mount' and, for that

reason, inaccurately describe themselves as 'christians.' Such equivocal terminology is to-day so dangerous that it is worth emphasising the truism that the 'sermon' is the epitome of pre-christian morality. (The famous 'golden rule,' for example,—" Do unto others as you would they should do unto you "—was a commonplace of Rabbinical teaching and, outside Judaism, at least as old as Confucius.) As Bishop Thomas Strong put it in his *Christian Ethics*, the 'Sermon' " takes its place rather with the older dispensation than with the new. It is still a law; it still gives commands to the will and sets before it an ideal. The will is left to find its own way to this perfect type; no guidance, no direct promise of guidance is given. So the Sermon on the Mount kills, to use St. Paul's language, as relentlessly as the Law . . . The Greek ethical system, the Jewish Law, the Sermon on the Mount, have all this one character in common—that they command from without."

Superseding and abolishing all such commands was the new and unique ' Do this.' A personal relationship with God and a power to do his will replaced human aspirations after goodness expressed in ideal codes of conduct. For those from whom the gift of faith might be withheld or those who by circumstances could have no knowledge of the New Covenant, the way of salvation still lay—and lies—in obedience to the Old. But ' the law and the prophets,' though endorsed by Jesus, are not specifically his commandments and stand on a different footing from his own ' Do this ' and the other two commands which are inextricably related to it—the command to be baptized and the command to love to the death fellow-sharers of the Meal: " A new commandment I give unto you that ye love one another as I have loved you." Because of baptism, making clean from sin,[1] the Christian may dare to partake of the meal; because of the partaking, he is bound in a unique way to the other partakers. "The Church," Péguy once said, "is a city. The bad citizen belongs to the city; the good stranger does not."

The Eucharist—to give the Meal the name which it has had since the first century—is thus in every way central not only to the life of the Church but to the understanding of Christianity. To know the prayer which accompanies the action is to know the Faith.

And the Faith is the faith of whole, undivided Church, before schisms had sundered it. The formula of the Eucharistic Prayer—the 'Canon of the Mass,' as it is more usually called —has not varied since the end of the sixth century. Its final form was given to it by Gregory the Great, the Pope who sent Augustine to England. The Prayer as Augustine prayed it in that first Communion he celebrated in the ruined church of St. Martin in Canterbury in 597 is, word for word, the same prayer as has been said this particular morning at every Catholic altar all over the world.

Thus the Canon to-day is not only the prayer of unity within the Church itself. It is the potential point of unity for all those separated from the Church. The sects which have sprung up since the Reformation could all unite in saying the Canon. There *can* be nothing in the doctrine implied there from which any presbyterian or congregationalist or methodist could dissent, for no dissenter disagrees with the Catholic

---

[1] The sacrament of absolution necessary before every Communion is best understood as the extension of the sacrament of baptism in its aspect of cleansing.

Church on the question of the original Christianity St. Augustine brought to England. There is in the Canon only the teaching of the primitive Church (for, of course, Gregory the Great only put the final touches to prayers which had slowly developed or hardened into particular forms from apostolic times) and nothing whatever of 'late mediæval accretions' against which the Reformers inveighed. The Canon had already been in use, in its present form, for six hundred years *before* 'Transubstantiation' was defined in 1215.

In praying the Canon we unite ourselves with all fellow-christians 'throughout all ages, world without end.' In knowing the Canon, we become grounded in the teaching of the primitive Church which Protestants no less than Catholics accept and so we may find that the Lord's Table, despite all the controversies which have disgraced His followers, is indeed the centre of unity. And in knowing about the Canon, we can detect the false arguments of those opponents of the Faith who have tried and who still try to perpetuate disunity.

Because one of the reasons for their success is the unfamiliarity of non-catholics with the form in which Mass is now said, a few paragraphs will be given to the vestments and gestures of the priest. Though strictly outside the subject of the book, (which does not pretend to be a liturgical guide,) they may be of some use to those who, studying the prayers of the Canon, may wish to go to join in it when it is said in church but are deterred by what they have heard described as 'outlandish vestments' and 'meaningless gestures.' Even some of the Catholic laity are not, perhaps, altogether conversant with symbolisms which have become second-nature to their priests and may find, in the vesting-prayers, a new preparation for approaching the Canon itself, the Great Prayer which, more surely than any other prayer in the world, is the way to Him.

(i) *The Vestments of the Priest*

In the earliest Christian centuries, the celebrant at the Supper wore no special dress, though it is probable that, in the service of God and for his glory, he officiated in his best clothes. Gradually, through the years, that ' best dress ' at the altar came to be kept and reserved for that occasion only and, by the end of the fourth century, St. Jerome could explain: " The Holy Religion has one dress for Divine Service and another for everyday use," for " we ought not to enter the Holy of Holies in soiled everyday clothes, but with a clean conscience and clean clothes to administer the mysteries of the Lord."

Secular fashions changed, but the ' altar clothes ' remained the same. They are still, in essence, the same. ' Mass vestments ' are only the ' stylised ' dress of the ordinary first-century layman in the Roman Empire. Allowing for modifications for utility and glorifications for devotion, every priest still puts on, before he goes to the altar, the clothes of Christ. And, as he dons each one, he says a prayer[1] which points the symbolic value which has gathered round them down the centuries. To those who can read the language, the figure at the altar is literally clothed in prayer.

The Amice

The amice, the first garment the priest puts on, is a large linen 'kerchief which originated in the Rome of the third

[1] Though these prayers are later developments.

century B.C. and was worn as to-day one might wear a scarf under an overcoat. Eventually it falls back, like a large white collar, over the other vestments; but, while he is actually vesting, the priest keeps it over his head, somewhat in the manner in which women wear scarves. The effect is that of a helmet and it is that thought, precisely—the 'helmet of salvation' of St. Paul's catalogue of the armour of Christ—which underlies the prayer:

Place, O Lord, the helmet of salvation upon my head that I may overcome the assaults of the Devil.
(Impone, Domine, capiti meo galeam salutis, ad expugnandos diabolicos incursus.)

The Alb

Next comes the alb, the sleeved garment of white linen which reaches to the ground. As the *tunica manicata alba* (the 'white tunic with sleeves') or the *tunica talaris* (the 'tunic reaching to the ankles'), it was the common dress of the Empire in the days of Christ, having gradually evolved from the short sleeveless 'chiton' universally worn by the Greeks of the first six centuries B.C. .

As early as A.D. 320 it had been laid down that the tunica talaris should be worn by deacons at the altar and by A.D. 589 —seven years before St. Augustine's coming to England— a Council of the Church recognised it as an 'official' dress and enacted that " neither deacon nor subdeacon shall presume to put off his alba till after Mass is over.".

Symbolically the alb, with its whiteness and its size, has

become a figure of integrity and the prayer said at its putting-on recalls that picture in the Apocalypse of the redeemed in heaven " which came out of great tribulation and have washed their robes and made them white in the blood of the Lamb."

> Cleanse me, O Lord, and purify my heart that, being made white in the blood of the Lamb, I may enjoy eternal happiness.
> (Dealba me, Domine, et munda cor meum: ut in sanguine Agni dealbatus, gaudiis perfruar sempiternis.)

The last phrase is, of course, an epitome of the promised reward to those who, through great tribulation, kept their integrity: "They shall hunger no more, neither thirst any more; neither shall the sun light on them or any heat; for the Lamb which is in the midst of the throne shall feed them and shall lead them unto living fountains of water; and God shall wipe away all tears from their eyes."

The Girdle

The girdle which confines the loose-fitting alb round the waist retains for christians the symbolism which it already possessed in the pagan world:

> Gird me, O Lord, with the girdle of purity and extinguish in me the fire of lust that the virtue of continence and chastity may ever abide in me.
> (Praecinge me, Domine, cingulo puritatis, et exstingue in lumbis meis humorem libidinis: ut maneat in· me virtus continentiae et castitatis.)

The Maniple

A Roman slave, waiting at table, carried over his left arm a *mappa*, a plain linen napkin for guests to wipe their hands on after a meal (the secular descendant and near-equivalent is the waiter's napkin) and, in the Church, from the earliest times, a piece of white linen was attached to the priest's left wrist for wiping the communion vessels and his hands at celebrations of the Eucharist. This 'maniple,' even as late as the twelfth century, was still sometimes of linen and was so used; though, centuries earlier, it had in general become a decorated and embroidered strip of silk or other stuff. A similar transition from utility to ceremonial had, in fact, taken place in non-christian Rome, for the *mappa* wrapped round the left fore-arm was also a magisterial badge of importance, used by the consul or praetor to give the sign for the start of a chariot-race in the circus.

Whatever the maniple's outward transformations, however, it never lost its inward meaning of service and still it indicates the priest as the servant of the altar. And, in the prayer, this thought of labour—even of slave-labour and its weariness—is unequivocally stressed:

May I be worthy, O Lord, so to bear the maniple of tears and sorrow that with joy I may receive the reward of my labour.

(Merear, Domine, portare manipulum fletues et doloris: ut cum exsultatione recipiam mercedem laboris.)

The Stole

Larger than the *mappa* but used for much the same practical purpose was the *orarium* (derived from *os, oris,* face, and having no connection with *orate,* to pray), a linen cloth for wiping the face, which was a common part of the dress of Romans of all classes. At first it was worn round the neck and later over the shoulder—as a bathing-towel to-day may be carried in either position. Originally about the size of a towel—about fifty by thirty inches—it later became reduced in width to about four inches and increased in length to anything from eight to ten feet. By this change into a long band, it lost its utility, but not its significance. Though its appearance now is of a magnificently embroidered strip which the priest wears round his neck with the ends falling below his waist, its unforgotten origin is the ' towel ' which Jesus used at the Last Supper to wipe after He had washed the disciples' feet. And the prayer of the stole—as the *orarium* came to be called— recalls his: " What I do thou knowest not now, but thou shalt know hereafter . . . If I wash thee not, thou hast no part with me."

> Restore to me, O Lord, the stole of immortality, which I lost by the transgression of the first parent: and although unworthy, as I draw near to thy sacred mystery, may I be found worthy of everlasting joy.
> (Redde mihi, Domine, stolam immortalitatis, quam perdidi in prevaricatione primi parentis: et quamvis indignus accedo ad tuum sacrum mysterium, merear tamen gaudium sempiternum.)

INTRODUCTION

The Chasuble

There is one garment—and that, perhaps, the best known—of the Roman Empire which is not represented among the Eucharistic vestments. There is no trace of the toga; for the toga, as the distinctive dress of those who were legally Roman citizens, was beyond the reach of many, if not most, of the early Christians. Paul, indeed, might have worn it; but not Peter: Pilate, but not Christ. But all could have worn the *paenula* or *casula*—the ' cloak ' which Paul left at Troy. This large garment of conical shape, reaching practically to the feet all round (its name *casula* means ' tent '), was used by all classes except the Emperor, who eschewed it because it was so commonplace. Even those who had a right to the toga sometimes substituted the *casula* for it and, as time went on, officials wore it even on state occasions. It thus acquired a character of importance and for Christians became the obvious garment for priests at the altar. It has remained, as the chasuble, the distinctive vestment of the Mass, worn at no other time and by no one but the officiating priest.

For reasons of utility, the chasuble soon shrunk in size, though the memory of the days when it was still heavy and tent-like is still recalled at High Mass when the deacon raises the chasuble (for no practical reason now, though then it was a necessity) to allow free play to the celebrant's arms when censing the altar and elevating the Host and Chalice. And its all-enveloping character is remembered, too, in the symbolism of the vesting-prayer—for the chasuble betokens that charity with which a christian must be clothed and which makes the yoke of Christ easy and his burden light:

O Lord, who hast said: My yoke is easy and My burden is light, make me so able to bear it that I may obtain Thy grace. Amen.

(Domine, qui dixiste: Jungum meum suavum est, et onus meum leve: fac, ut istud portare sic valeam, quod consequar tuam gratiam. Amen.)

So, with the ' Amen,' the priest stands fully vested—an anonymity in clothes which are a parable, proclaiming to the people whom he represents before God that he and they must approach the Table of the Lord with intellects guarded against the wisdom of the serpent, with personalities sharpened to an integrity of will, with emotions guarded against the looseness of lust: humble in service, yet certain of a rewarding heaven opened to them by the one atoning death. And, above all things, charity.

(ii) The Sign of the Cross

" We should make the sign of the cross with great reverence," said the Curé d'Ars. " We begin with the head—that is, the *chief*, the creation, the Father: then the heart, love, life, redemption, the Son; then the shoulders, strength, the holy Ghost." Because Christ on the cross redeemed all and through the cross sanctifies each, the making of the sign of the cross is, in its simplicity, more eloquent than oratory and what was once the secret communication between outcasts in imperial Rome has become a recognised signature for many occasions —formally, as it were a key to a silent sanctuary, before and after prayer; joyfully, as a blessing, to betoken the fullness of God's mercy; pleadingly, for strength and protection in danger and temptation. Perhaps to non-catholic Englishmen, its use is epitomised when it is made on a child's forehead at baptism: "We receive this child into the congregation of Christ's flock and do sign him with the sign of the Cross in token that hereafter he shall not be ashamed to confess the faith of Christ crucified and manfully to fight under his banner against sin, the world and the devil; and to continue Christ's faithful soldier and servant unto his life's end."

During the Canon of the Mass, the sign of the cross is made twenty-six times. It is almost as if the Church were determined that, however attention may wander and words become a mechanical repetition, however dry the devotion or lazy the intellect, the body at least shall focus the meaning. A stranger, totally ignorant of Christianity, would, merely by watching the gestures accompanying the Canon, know that the prayer concerned a Cross.

Yet the signs are not repetitive. The twenty-six fall into six separate groups each having its own particular significance. In the first prayer, the *Te Igitur*, when the offerings of bread and wine which represent us ourselves are dedicated to God, a three-fold cross is made over them. Here it is a reminder that the God to Whom we are praying is a Trinity; it is an indication, by the hands, of the gifts themselves and it is an emphasis that only through the Cross can we make any offering at all.

The *Quam Oblationem* immediately before the Consecration and the *Unde et memores* immediately after it each contains a five-fold cross, symbolising the five wounds of Christ. The last signature on the bread and wine, they are the first on the

Body and Blood. As the nail-prints and the spear-thrust were, so to speak, the sign-manual of the sacrifice, authenticating that the resurrected Body which had experienced death was indeed the same that had hung, so pierced, on the Cross—" Reach hither thy hand and thrust it into my side "—, so this symbolising of those wounds bridges another mystical transition. And at the Consecration itself the sign of the cross is made twice at the word " bless " as the nárrative of the Last Supper recalls that Jesus blessed the bread before he broke it and the cup before he gave it to his disciples.

After the Consecration there are two groups of three and one of five crosses. In the *Supplices*, the priest follows the thought of the prayer as it moves from consecration to communion. Having kissed the altar, he makes the sign over the offerings and on himself (as representing the congregation) as he asks that all who partake at the altar of the sacred Body and Blood may be filled with every heavenly blessing and grace.

The *Per quem*, in which Christ is spoken of as creating, blessing, sanctifying, quickening and bestowing on us every good thing was originally a simple blessing-formula and the three-fold cross here is the ordinary gesture of blessing; but in the prayer which immediately follows it, the *Per ipsum*— the ' great Doxology '—the five-fold cross is alive with profound and varied theological meaning.

At this point in the Canon, in the days of Gregory the Great, the deacon lifted above his head the two-handled Chalice while the celebrant elevated the consecrated Bread and with it touched the side of the Chalice, to signify the unity of the two elements in the one sacrament. " Their movements coincided and fused in a single gesture of offering which was the most striking comment upon the Doxology. Of this rite we have kept the conjunction of the two species, during which the five signs of the cross are made, followed by their simultaneous elevation."

Here the five crosses are made with the Host Itself. The full number, once more, memorialises Christ's wounds, but by dividing them into a three and a two, a further symbolism is added. The first three, made from lip to lip of the Chalice, recall again in thought the Holy Trinity; the last two, made between the Chalice and the breast of the celebrant, betoken not only a survival of the very ancient Christian idea that, as Eve sprang from the side of Adam asleep, so the Church sprang from the side of Christ in the sleep of death on the Cross, but also the extension of Christ, through the Church, to the whole world in fulfilment of his promise that, uplifted on the cross, He would draw all things to Himself.

So the twenty-six signs of the cross in the Canon become, rightly understood, the very reverse of a repetitive gesture or a mechanical action. Together they form a mute commentary of devotion in the silence of the Great Prayer.

THE
CANON OF THE MASS

THE GREAT PRAYER

THE TE IGITUR

Te igitur, clementissime Pater, per Jesum Christum Filium tuum Dominum nostrum, supplices rogamus acpetimus, uti accepta habeas et benedicas, haec dona, haec munera, haec sancta sacrificia illibata,

In primis, quae tibi offerimus pro Ecclesia tua sancta catholica: quam pacificare, custodire, adunare, et regere digneris toto orbe terrarum: una cum famulo tuo Papa nostro, N., et Antistite nostro, N. et omnibus orthodoxis atque catholicae, et apostolicae fidei cultoribus.

THE MEMENTO DOMINE

Memento, Domine, famulorum famularumque tuarum N. et N. et omnium circumstantium, quorum tibi fides cognita est, et nota devotio; pro quibus tibi offerimus, vel qui tibi offerunt hoc sacrificium laudis, pro se, suisque omnibus; pro redemptione animarum suarum, pro spe salutatis, et incolumitatis suae: tibique reddunt vota sua aeterno Deo, vivo et vero.

THE COMMUNICANTES

Communicantes et memoriam venerantes, in primis gloriosae semper Virginis Mariae, Genetricis Dei et Domini nostri Jesu Christi: sed et beatorum Apostolorum ac Martyrum tuorum, Petri et Pauli, Andreae, Jacobi, Joannis, Thomae, Jacobi, Philippi, Bartolomaei, Matthaei, Simonis et Thaddaei, Leni, Cleti, Clementis, Xysti, Cornelii, Cypriani, Laurentii, Chrysogoni, Joannis et Pauli, Cosmae et Damiani, et omnium Sanctorum tuorum; quorum meritis precibusque concedas, ut in omnibus protectionis tuae muniamur auxilio. Per eumdem Christum Dominum nostrum. Amen.

Therefore we pray and beseech Thee, most merciful Father, through Jesus Christ Thy Son, our Lord, that thou wouldst vouchsafe to accept and bless these gifts, these offerings, these holy and unblemished sacrifices,

Which in the first place we offer up to Thee for Thy holy Catholic Church that it may please Thee to grant her peace, to protect, unite and govern her throughout the world, together with Thy servant, N. our Pope, N. our Bishop and all true believers and professors of the Catholic and Apostolic Faith.

Be mindful, O Lord, of Thy servants, men and women, N. and N., and of all who are present here, whose faith and devotion are known to Thee (for whom we offer, or) who offer up to Thee this sacrifice of praise for themselves, their families and friends; for the redemption of their souls, for the hope of their security and salvation and for which they now pay their vows to Thee, the eternal, living and true God.

Joining in communion with and venerating the memory in the first place of the glorious and ever-virgin Mary, Mother of our God and Lord Jesus Christ; as also of Thy blessed apostles and martyrs, Peter and Paul, Andrew, James, John, Thomas, James, Philip, Bartholomew, Matthew, Simon and Thaddeus (Jude); Linus, Cletus, Clement, Sixtus, Cornelius, Cyprian, Lawrence, Chrysogonus, John and Paul, Cosmas and Damian, and of all Thy saints, by whose merits and prayers grant that we may be defended by the help of Thy protection, through the same Christ our Lord. Amen.

THE GREAT PRAYER

THE HANC IGITUR

Hanc igitur oblationem servitutis nostrae, sed et cunctae familiae tuae, quaesumus, Domine, ut placatus accipias: diesque nostros in tua pace disponas, atque ab aeterna damnatione nos eripi, et in electorum tuorum jubeas grege numerari. Per Christum Dominum nostrum. Amen.

THE QUAM OBLATIONEM

Quam oblationem tu Deus in omnibus, quaesumus, benedictam, adscriptam, ratam, rationabilem acceptabilemque facere digneris; ut nobis Corpus et Sanguis fiat dilectissimi Filii tui Domini nostri Jesu Christi,

THE QUI PRIDIE

Qui pridie quam pateretur, accepit panem in sanctas ac venerabiles manus suas: et elevatis oculis in caelum ad te, Deum Patrem suum omnipotentem, tibi gratias agens, benedixit fregit, deditque discipulis suis, dicens: Accipite et manducate ex hoc omnes. Hoc est enim Corpus Meum.

Simili modo postquam coenatum est, accipiens et hunc praeclarum Calicem in sanctas ac venerabiles manus suas: item tibi gratias agens, benedixit deditque discipulis suis, dicens: Accipite et bibite ex eo omnes. Hic est enim Calix Sanguinis mei, novi et aeterni testamenti: mysterium fidei: qui pro vobis et pro multis effundetur in remissionem peccatorum.

Haec quotienscumque feceritis, in mei memoriam facietis.

We therefore beseech Thee, O Lord, graciously to accept this offering which we, Thy servants, and Thy whole family make unto Thee; and to order our days in Thy peace and to deliver us from eternal damnation and to number us in the flock of Thine elect. Through Christ our Lord. Amen.

Which oblation do Thou, O God, vouchsafe in all respects to make blessed, approved, ratified, reasonable and acceptable, that it may be made for us the Body and Blood of Thy most beloved Son Jesus Christ our Lord,

Who, the day before He suffered, took bread into His holy and adorable hands and, with His eyes raised to Heaven, unto Thee, God, His Almighty Father, giving thanks to Thee, He blessed, broke and gave it to His disciples, saying: Take and eat ye all of this. This is My Body.

In like manner, after supper, taking this precious Chalice into His holy and adorable hands, and giving thanks to Thee, He blessed it and gave to His disciples, saying: Take and drink ye all of this, for this is the Chalice of My Blood, of the new and eternal Covenant: the mystery of faith: which shall be shed for you and for many for the remission of sins.

As often as ye shall do these things, ye shall do them in remembrance of Me.

THE UNDE ET MEMORES

Unde et memores, Domine, nos servi tui, sed et plebs tua sancta, ejusdem Christi Filii tui Domini nostri tam beatae Passionis, nec non et ab inferis Resurrectionis, sed et in caelos gloriosiae Ascensionis: offerimus praeclarae majestati tuae de tuis donis ac datis, Hostiam puram, Hostiam sanctam, Hostiam immaculatam, Panem sanctum vitae aeternae, et Calicem salutis perpetuae.

THE SUPRA QUAE

Supra quae propitio ac sereno vultu respicere digneris, et accepta habere, sicuti accepta habere dignatus es munera pueri tui justi Abel, et sacrificium Patriarchae nostri Abrahae: et quod tibi obtulit summus sacerdos tuus Melchisedech, sanctum sacrificium, immaculatam hostiam.

THE SUPPLICES

Supplices te rogamus, omnipotens Deus: jube haec preferri per manus sancti Angeli tui in sublime altare tuum, in conspectu divinae majestatis tuae: ut quotquot ex hac altaris participatione sacrosanctum Filii tui Corpus et Sanguinem sumpserimus, omni benedictione coelesti et gratia repleamur. Per undem Christum Dominum nostrum. Amen.

Wherefore, O Lord, we Thy servants, as also Thy holy people, calling to mind (making an *anamnesis* of) the blessed Passion of Christ Thy Son our Lord, as also His Resurrection from the dead and His glorious Ascension into Heaven, offer unto Thine excellent Majesty from what Thou hast Thyself given and granted, a Sacrifice that is pure, that is holy, that is unblemished—the holy Bread of eternal life and the Chalice of everlasting salvation.

Upon which vouchsafe to look with a kind and serene countenance and to accept them, even as Thou didst graciously hold accepted the gifts of Thy just servant Abel, the sacrifice of our Patriarch Abraham and that which Thy high priest Melchisedech offered to Thee, a holy sacrifice, an unblemished victim.

We most humbly beseech Thee, almighty God, to command that these things be carried up by the hands of Thy holy angel to Thine altar on high, in the sight of Thy divine majesty, that so many of us as are partakers of the precious Body and Blood of Thy Son at this altar may be filled with all heavenly benediction and grace. Through the same Christ our Lord. Amen.

THE MEMENTO ETIAM

Memento etiam, Domine, famulorum, famularumque tuarum N. et N., qui nos praecesserunt cum signo fidei et dormiunt in somno pacis. Ipsis, Domine, et omnibus in Christo quiescentibus locum refrigerii, lucis et pacis, ut indulgeas, deprecamur, per eundem Christum Dominum nostrum. Amen.

THE NOBIS QUOQUE PECCATORIBUS

Nobis quoque peccatoribus famulis tuis, de multitudine miserationum tuarum sperantibus, partem aliquam, et societatem donare digneris, cum tuis sanctis Apostolis, et Martyribus: cum Joanne, Stephano, Matthia, Barnaba, Ignatio, Alexandro, Marcellino, Petro, Felicitate, Perpetua, Agatha, Lucia, Agnete, Caecilia, Anastasia, et omnibus Sanctis tuis: intra quorum nos consortium, non aestimator meriti, sed veniae, quaesumus, largitor admitte, per Christum Dominum nostrum.

THE PER QUEM HAEC OMNIA

Per quem haec omnia, Domine, semper bona creas, sanctificas, vivificas, benedicis, et praestas nobis.

THE PER IPSUM

Per ipsum et cum ipso et in ipso, est tibi, Deo Patri omnipotenti, in unitate Spiritus Sancti, omnis honor et gloria, per omnia saecula saeculorum.

Be mindful, O Lord, of Thy servants, men and women, N. and N., who have gone before us with the sign of faith and sleep the sleep of peace. To them, O Lord, and to all who rest in Christ, grant, we beseech Thee a place of refreshing, light and peace, through the same Christ our Lord. Amen.

To us sinners also, Thy servants, trusting in the multitude of Thy mercies, vouchsafe to grant some part and fellowship with Thy holy Apostles and Martyrs: with John, Stephen, Matthias, Barnabas, Ignatius, Alexander, Marcellinus, Peter, Felicity, Perpetua, Agatha, Lucy, Agnes, Cecilia, Anastasia, and with all Thy Saints, within whose fellowship we beseech Thee to admit us, not weighing our merit, but pardoning our offences, through Christ our Lord.

By whom, O Lord, all these good things Thou dost ever create, sanctify, quicken, bless and bestow on us.

Through Him and with Him and in Him, be unto Thee, O God the Father Almighty, in the unity of the Holy Ghost, all honour and glory, world without end.

THE TE IGITUR

Therefore we pray and beseech Thee, most merciful Father, through Jesus Christ Thy Son, our Lord, that Thou wouldst vouchsafe to accept and bless these gifts, these offerings, these holy and unblemished sacrifices,

Which in the first place we offer up to Thee for Thy holy Catholic Church that it may please Thee to grant her peace, to protect, unite and govern her throughout the world, together with Thy servant, N. our Pope, N. our Bishop and all true believers and professors of the Catholic and Apostolic Faith.

Te igitur, clementissime Pater, per Jesum Christum Filium tuum Dominum nostrum, supplices rogamus ac petimus, uti accepta habeas et benedicas, haec dona, haec munera, haec sancta sacrificia illibata,

In primis, quae tibi offerimus pro Ecclesia tua sancta catholica: quam pacificare, custodire, adunare, et regere digneris toto orbe terrarum: una cum famulo tuo Papa nostro, N., et antistite nostro, N., et omnibus orthodoxis atque catholicae, et apostolicae fidei cultoribus.

THE CANON starts with the word ' therefore,' linking it to the *Sursum Corda* (a dialogue-chant) and the *Preface* which mark the beginning of the Mass of the Faithful. The congregation has expressed itself in praise, penitence and prayer; the sacred scriptures, epistle and gospel, have been read; the sermon, expounding the gospel, has been preached;

the Nicene Creed, that hymn of faith which is also an intellectual assertion of unity of belief, has been sung; and, with it, the Mass of the Catechumens has ended. At this point, in the primitive centuries, the church was emptied of all but those who had the right to receive communion. No unbaptised person, no jewish or pagan visitor, was allowed to be present at the Liturgy of the Supper.

After their departure and when, on the holy table, had been laid the offerings of bread and wine, the priest called to the faithful—as he still does—to lift their hearts to heaven and to ' make eucharist ' (to give thanks) as was very meet, right and their bounden duty at all times and in all places.

The train of thought is " It is right for us to give thanks, *therefore* we ask you to receive our offering " and if the difference of words in English a little obscures the classical identity—for the Latin oblatio (offering) is the earliest christian translation of the Greek eucharistia (thanksgiving)—yet still the thought overtops the tongue, for, in the universal language of action, gratitude is evinced by a gift.

On the question of language, it is perhaps worth notice, in passing, that in the opening section of the *Te igitur*, the literary style of the Canon is epitomised. The actual author is unknown, though it is possible that he was Firmicus Maternus, a Christian writer of the fourth century whose great work, *Concerning the Errors of Non-Christian Religions* is an invaluable historical source for the passwords, formulae and ceremonies of the pagan mysteries of Eleusis, Isis and—particularly—Mithra. But whoever he was he had a recognisably individual style. As Jungmann, in his *Mass of the Roman Rite*, says of the author's stylistic peculiarities: " He has a preference for word-doubles—rogamus ac petimus; accepta habeas et benedicas; catholicae et apostolicae fidei; quorum fides cognita est et nota devotio; sanctas et venerabiles manus; de tuis donis ac datis . . . non aestimator meriti sed veniae largitor; omnis honor et gloria . . . Sometimes he employs a three-member phrase and in the petition for the consecration and in the prayer of blessing before the closing doxology, there are even five members."

Here, at the outset, are 'pray and beseech,' 'accept and bless' and 'these gifts, these offerings, these holy and unblemished sacrifices.' But the repetitions are not merely a stylistic balance. Each word is a *mot juste*. The 'asking' is no casual or conventional thing, yet the casual and conventional word *rogare*, weakened by the currency of everyday speech, has to be used. To give it a meaning proportionate to its context the stronger 'beseech,' *petere*, is called in for emphasis: and so the atmosphere of urgency is defined. In 'accept' and 'bless,' a similar force is seen, though the very word 'accept' has to-day a new life in that it challenges the comfortable assumptions of a world unaccustomed to the language of sacrifice.

petimus?

(i) Sacrifice,

In popular theology, much misunderstanding could be avoided if only the word 'atonement' were pronounced as it is meant, 'at-one-ment,' the making-at-one, and the word 'sacrifice' etymologically remembered as 'something made sacred.'[1] So many fantasies of bloodthirsty gods and benighted

---

[1] 'Safe' and 'sane' come from the same root.

much is lost when the Mass is reduced to merely a communal meal; as has been the tendency over the last 50-60 years men have gathered round the words that a simple analogy is permissible.

A child, having displeased its parents by its naughtiness, wishes to be at-one again, to heal the rift which (it feels) has been made. Atonement is a necessity, though, in fact, there is no break in the parents' love. As a token it gives to the parents its most treasured possession—an old doll, perhaps, or a new train. The thing is of no value in itself and, as the parents have been the original donors, it is not even, in one sense, a gift. But because it is precious to the child who sets it apart and offers it—sacrifices it—it is of inestimable value as the outward and visible sign of the ' broken and contrite heart.' It is (in technical language) the *ritual* sacrifice betokening the *real* sacrifice which is the submission of heart and will. With the parents' acceptance of it, ' at-one-ment ' is achieved.

It is not, however, unknown for certain children, having discovered that this method of reconciliation ' works,' automatically to fall back on it in any crisis. Wise parents, in such cases, refuse to accept the gift. They know that the token has become a trick and that behind the gesture there is something less than love and integrity.

Thus, for a true sacrifice, it is not enough for some precious thing to be offered. It must also be accepted; for it is the acceptance, not the offering, that is the guarantee of genuineness. " Though I give my body to be burned and have not charity, it profiteth me nothing." The prayer for acceptance, which opens the Canon, is thus a recurring *motif*: and here, at the outset, when on the altar is the bread which represents the sacrifice of ourselves, the need for acceptance is immediately admitted. ' Accept ' is the word first not only in order but in importance.

But the bread and wine are more than gifts to be accepted; they are offerings and sacrifices to be blessed—offerings because they betoken thanksgiving, sacrifices because they are set apart in a special way. As we ask God, through Christ the eternal Sacrifice, to accept, so we ask him, through Christ the eternal Priest, to bless.

(We are not of course asking that God will accept and bless the offering of our Lord's Body and Blood, for of this we have no doubt. Christ was received once and for all at his Ascension. We are remembering that we, represented by our gifts—not now brought directly, as in the Church's early years, but bought from the money we have given in the collection— are to be transformed into Christ and, so, offered to God.)

In this opening petition, moreover, we show " that our intentions are already expanding into the intentions of Christ; that we have begun to put on His all-embracing sympathy with mankind; that there is an identity of purpose between our oblation and His." That, in making this offering in the first place on behalf of the whole Church, we are indeed identifying our intention with Christ's may be realised very simply by remembering the verse of a hymn now so hackneyed that the thought behind the words is often over-looked:

> The Church's one foundation
> Is Jesus Christ, her Lord;
> She is His new creation
> By water and the Word.

From heaven He came and sought her,
  To be His holy Bride.
With His own Blood He bought her
  And for her life He died.

But what is the Church for which He died—" Christ's
Catholic known Church" as St. Thomas More loved to
call her?

(ii) *The Church*

From this point, for the remainder of the *Te igitur* and
through the next two prayers, *Memento Domine* and *Communicantes*, is given a definition of the Church that is without
an equal. If, at first sight, it may seem as stark as a catalogue,
that may be because such precision is essential to understanding
that the Church, the Mystical Body of Christ, does indeed
reveal, as did Christ in his Incarnate Body, the principle of
particularity. At any moment in time the Church is definable
and exclusive—this, not that—just as, during His lifetime on
earth, Jesus, when He was teaching at Capernaum, was not in
Jerusalem or, when He was praying on a mountainside, was
inaccessible to the crowds seeking Him in the streets.

This truism tends to be evaded by those who like to think
of 'the Church' as an inchoate mass of the 'spiritually
minded' everywhere. Few evasions are more deadly to the
understanding of the Christian religion, though the dislike of
precision has usually a kindly motive for, by a further confusion
of thought, a refusal to define becomes equated with an
assertion of universality. But, of course, it is not. To say

that ' this ' is, is not to deny that ' that ' may be. No one dare limit the mercy of God; no one may assert that any human soul is lost; no one may say that, for those outside the defined Church, God and salvation are inaccessible—a basic truth summed up in the well-known sentence: " We are bound by the sacraments, but God is not." But, in practice, it is perhaps wiser to put the sentence the other way round: " God is not bound by the sacraments—but we are."

Of the thirty-three years of Jesus's life on earth we have recorded for us, when every incident is included, a space of time equal to a few months. What He did, whom He met, where He went during the rest of the time we neither know nor can know. We can assert that He spoke to Pilate; we cannot deny that He may have spoken to Herod. But it is for us to accept and try to understand what is, rather than to insist on our right profitlessly to speculate on what may have been. As with the incarnate, so with the mystical Body. The Church is a particularity—as definable as Noah's Ark, which is its fore-type—a recognisable human organisation as well as a divine organism.

For this chosen and sacramental community, before proceeding to the exact definition of it, the *Te Igitur* asks first the basic necessities of every community—safety against outside enemies, unity within itself and the government which is the guarantee of ordered development. " Guard, unite and govern." In asking God for these, we echo Christ's own prayer for the Church at the Last Supper: " Holy Father, keep through thine own name those whom thou hast given me, that they may be one, as we are . . . I have given them thy word; and the world hath hated them, because they are not of the world, even as I am not of the world. I pray not that thou shouldest take them out of the world, but that thou shouldest keep them from the evil . . . Neither pray I for these alone, but for them also which shall believe on me through their word; that they may all be one; as thou, Father, art in me and I in thee, that they also may be one in us: that the world may believe that thou hast sent me. And the glory which thou gavest me I have given them; that they may be one, even as we are one: I in them and thou in me that they may be made perfect in one."

And once the particularity is accepted, universality follows. Always, in the Christian religion, that is the order. It is part of the logic of the Incarnation. For St. John Chrysostom, the *Te igitur* is ' the common and universal ' prayer—a fact on which Maurice Zundel makes the memorable comment in *The Splendour of the Liturgy* that it " embraces the entire world in the universal motherhood of the Church. From the unity of its scope no soul is excluded . . . The Mass is for all as God is for all. Those who do not recognise to-day will perhaps recognise to-morrow the face of the Mother whose prayer embraced them even before their birth, and in their turn will enter the visible unity, thus fulfilling one of the sublimest duties of humanity redeemed and called to become mystically, in accordance with Love's mystical demands, one single person in Jesus."

(iii) *The Pope and the Bishops*

The *Preface*, on the feasts of Apostles, is in this form: " It is very meet, right and our bounden duty that we, O Lord, should humbly pray that Thou, the Eternal Shepherd, wouldst not forsake Thy flock but, through Thy holy Apostles, wouldst keep a continual watch over it that it may be governed by those self-same rulers whom Thou didst appoint in Thy stead as pastors of Thy people." It serves as a reminder that the Apostles themselves are still alive and still part of the Church, though, having fought the good fight, they have passed from that part which is militant on earth to that which is triumphant in heaven.

And on earth their successors have still the burden of government and the responsibility of the keys. To-day the Church Militant numbers its members in hundreds of millions, yet it still has organic identity, as an oak with an acorn, with the Church of a few hundreds which was entrusted to Peter.

It is unfortunate that in England the position of the Pope in the Church still arouses controversy. Article XXXVII of the Church of England, with its reminder that " the Bishop of Rome hath no jurisdiction in this realm of England "— a plain statement of fact which is equally applicable to any foreign ruler—has come somehow to imply that the Head of the Universal Church ought not to have *spiritual* juris-diction in England (which, by the nature of the case, he cannot avoid) and that ' the Bishop of Rome ' is not the head of the universal Church. It is enough to say that Archbishop Cranmer himself, the architect of Anglicanism, put this point into exact perspective when he explained the ' Royal Supremacy ' as meaning that " every king in his own realm is supreme head . . . Nero was Head of the Church, that is in worldly respect of the temporal bodies of men, of whom the Church consisteth: for so he beheaded Peter and the Apostles."

Yet more potent than political and theological niceties is the effect through the centuries of such books as *The Pilgrim's Progress*. Somewhere in the subconscious of the thousands who, in every generation, read it as children lurks the shadow of Giant Pope, surrounded by " the bones, blood, ashes etc." of his victims, though now " grown so crazy and stiff in his joints that he can do little more than sit in his cave's mouth, grinning at pilgrims as they go by, and biting his nails because he cannot come at them."

Irrational prejudices still cloud the reason and it would be foolish to ignore their existence even though, fortunately, the roar of 'No Popery' which once roused London mobs to murder has declined to little more than ecclesiastical special pleading. Nor is this the place to argue the matter of the primacy of Peter and his successors. Whatever his political feelings, every Christian can at least pray for the man on whose shoulders has fallen 'the care of all the churches.'[1] But one may surely ask whether, let us say, a Taoist, with no controversial axe to grind, would for one second dispute the overwhelming evidence. " Thou art Peter and upon this rock[2] I will build my church and the gates of Hell shall not prevail against it. And I will give unto thee the keys of Heaven and whatsoever thou shalt bind on earth shall be bound in heaven and whatsoever thou shalt loose on earth shall be loosed in Heaven ";—the appointment.

[1] When the Pope himself says Mass, he alters the words to ' me, thine unworthy servant.'

[2] This is, of course, a pun on his new-given name, *petros*, a rock. It is against the sense to interpret ' this rock ' as anything but Peter himself.

Then, after the Resurrection, Christ's three-fold charge to
him: "Feed my sheep," within a few days of which the
citizens of Jerusalem "brought forth their sick into the streets
and laid them on beds and couches that at least the shadow of
Peter passing by might overshadow some of them."

The early Christian centuries bear continual witness to the
primacy of Peter's successors in the Roman See. All Christian
roads led to Rome. "To Rome then journeyed," writes the
Anglican theologian, Dr. Trevor Jalland in his Bampton
Lectures on *The Church and the Papacy*, "Polycarp from
Smyrna; Valentinus from Egypt; Cerdo from Syria; Marc
from Sinope; Justin from Samaria; Tatian from Assyria;
Hegesippus from Jerusalem; Justin's pupils Euelpestus from
Cappadocia and Hierax from Phrygia; Rhodon, Irenaeus
and Florinus from Asia."

Throughout the course of history the story continues. Not
only in the ages of faith but in the later ages of doubt and
repudiation and revolt, Rome is central. Perhaps, even, the
Pope is seen most clearly as the 'sacrament of unity' when
all the forces of diverse rebellions are mustered against him.
In the swirl and eddy of the storm, we are most conscious of
the rock. And to-day what neutral observer if he were asked
who, under Christ, is Head of the Christian Church, would
not reply: "the Pope"?

Yet still those whispers of prejudice persist. Can they
perhaps be quietened a little by referring them to Peter himself? There have been weak Popes? Peter was a coward.
Foolish Popes? Peter was a very ordinary fisherman, misunderstanding much. Compromising Popes? Peter denied
Christ. Worldly Popes? Christ once said to Peter: "Get

thee behind me, Satan, for thou savourest not the things that be of God but the things that be of men," Power-loving Popes? Christ's answer to Peter, arguing with the others "which of them should be accounted the greatest" was "Behold, Satan hath desired to have you that he may sift you as wheat, but I have prayed for thee that thy faith fail not; and, when thou art converted, strengthen thy brethren."

And, in the last analysis, what is 'Papal Infallibility' but the certainty that Christ's prayer 'that thy faith fail not' was and is answered?

At the head of the Church, as an organisation, someone must stand. For nineteen centuries there has been no reasonable doubt as to his identity. Certainly there was no doubt in anyone's mind when Augustine at Canterbury prayed for "our Pope Gregory" who had sent him to bring the faith of Christ from Rome to the heathen English.

Next in the hierarchy of ruling come the other bishops. If the chief bishop is for all, the particular local bishop is for each. His true function, however organisational changes may have modified it as the Church has grown larger, is still essentially what it was in the primitive centuries when St. Cyprian could sum it up with: "These form a Church—the people united to their high priest and the flock following its shepherd; wherefore you must know that a bishop is constituted by his church and a church by its bishop."

As 'the man' of his church, the bishop stands on its behalf before God offering its corporate sacrifice by which 'it becomes what it is,' the Body of Christ. But he also stands on its behalf before the world proclaiming the revelation of God with which his particular church, the microcosm of 'the

Church,' is divinely charged. He is, as Dom Gregory Dix has expressed it in *The Apostolic Ministry*, " the creator of its lesser ministers; its representative to other churches; the administrator of its charity; the officer of its discipline; the centre of its unity; the hub of its whole, many-sided life, spiritual and temporal, inward and outward."

In this defining prayer, he is mentioned by name, as the Pope is mentioned by name. They are individual expressions of unity. But there is another unity—the remaining strand of the three-fold cord—to be remembered: that formed by the inter-relation of all the bishops. And so with this—" and for all true believers and professors of the Catholic Faith "[1] —the *Te igitur* ends.

[1] This is always understood—and, indeed, the context demands it—as referring to " all the Bishops in communion with the Church " rather than to the whole body of the faithful.

THE MEMENTO DOMINE

Be mindful, O Lord, of Thy servants, men and women, N. and
N., and of all who are present here, whose faith and devotion
are known to Thee (for whom we offer, or) who offer up to
Thee this sacrifice of praise for themselves, their families and
friends; for the redemption of their souls, for the hope of their
security and salvation and for which they now pay their vows
to Thee, the eternal, living and true God.

Memento, Domine, famulorum famularumque tuarum N. et N.
et omnium circumstantium, quorum tibi fides cognita est, et
nota devotio; pro quibus tibi offerimus, vel qui tibi offerunt hoc
sacrificium laudis, pro se, suisque omnibus; pro redemptione
animarum suarum, pro spe salutatis, et incolumitatis suae: tibique
reddunt vota sua aeterno Deo, vivo et vero.

IN ONE of his best-known poems, Rudyard Kipling reminded
us that

> God gave all men all earth to love,
>   But, since our hearts are small,
> Ordained for each one spot should prove
>   Beloved over all.

So with the Church-on-earth. And the thought of the Great

Prayer, after remembering the world-wide congregation bound through its pastors into a unity, answers experience and crystallises into the smallness of the known and loved. The first words of the *Memento Domine* are simply a prayer for our own living friends. All of it refers to the local church where we worship.

(i) *The Diptychs of the Living*

In origin, however, the moment when the priest joins his hands together to pray for ' N. and N.' was something other than this. It was the moment when the deacon went to the ambo—the raised desk or pulpit from which in the early basilicas the epistle and the gospel were chanted[1]—to read the Diptychs of the Living.

Diptychs, two writing-tablets hinged together, making a magnificent note-pad with an elaborately carved cover of ivory, wood or metal, were a common enough feature of Roman life. Consuls, at their installation in office, would often present them as souvenirs of the occasion to their friends; and wealthy private individuals adapted the custom to mark their own celebrations. One leaf of the finest of surviving diptychs (now in the Victoria and Albert Museum in South Kensington) commemorates, for example, a marriage between the Symmachi and the Nichomachi. It was natural, therefore, that diptychs should find their way into the service of the Church and in the early centuries, they were used for inscribing the names of benefactors and of those who provided the

---

[1] The word *ambo* is supposed to signify a mountain or elevation and Innocent III even cites, in connection with the deacon's reading of the Gospel, the text from Isaiah: " O Zion that bringeth good tidings, get thee up into a high mountain."

offertory gifts to the church, of those who were baptized and of the holy dead. But whether a baptismal register, a church roll, a list of bishops or a memorial of benefactors, they recorded none but Christians and exclusion from them was a penalty almost tantamount to excommunication.

Inevitably, even among the impeccably orthodox, worldly motives crept in and already at the end of the fourth century St. Jerome deplored the vanity of those who offered gifts in order to hear themselves publicly named by the deacon. Partly, perhaps, to counter this; partly because the actual bringing of gifts by the people gradually ceased and gave way to the present custom—the offering of money to provide gifts; partly because the list of names became too long, the reading of the diptychs ceased, although sometimes, at this point, they were laid on the altar. But the memory of the old custom is still preserved both in ritual action and in spoken formula. The alternative construction in the prayer " for whom we offer or who themselves offer " is a reminder that some who were named might not be able to be present, because, it might be, of sickness or travel, but that the gifts were still offered ' in their stead ' or ' for their intention.'[1] And at High Mass, when the Celebrant mentions softly the names of those for whom he prays, the Deacon, who is standing on his left, turns from him and walks a pace or two away. Though this is to ensure that he shall not overhear the Celebrant's names, and also may in quiet remember his own friends, it is also a relic of the days when the Deacon did in fact walk to the ambo for the reading of the public list.

The names are now matters of private concern, and the

---

[1] It does not mean that the Mass was being ' offered ' for them.

Celebrant's hands are joined, as in private prayer. The dis-
joining of them and the return to their ritual position at the
level of the shoulders—the position which betokens 'the
action of the Mass '—shows that the prayer is now ' for all
who are present here.'

The contrast of these two petitions, indicated by so simple
a gesture, is dramatic. First, every individual in the congregation detaches himself from the worshippers round him and
goes in thought to his own private world of love and friendship to bring, by prayer, those dear to him into the context
of this specific act of worship. Secondly, he identifies himself
with a particular gathering of men and women at one time
and in one place which, in all probability, will never be
exactly repeated. Both are essential aspects of the Church.
If we cannot pray the second prayer with the emotional warmth
we infuse into the first, we do not forget that it is no less an
expression of Christian love and unity. We may not know
any of those round us and we may not be particularly friendly
with those we do happen to know, but because they are all
together here, partakers of the same Sacrament, they con-
stitute the ' friends ' for whom, should occasion dictate, we
must, according to Christ's command, lay down our lives.
We can glimpse the meaning of the Christian paradox that
we must, with our will, love even those whom, with our
emotion, we cannot even manage to like.

(ii) The True Sacrifice

In the second half of the prayer is an outstanding example
of the allusiveness of the liturgy. The Fathers knew their

Bibles. The phrases ' sacrifice of praise ' and ' pay their vows '
are chosen with care and particularity from the fiftieth Psalm,
which is concerned with the mechanical sacrifices of the Law
in contradistinction to the true sacrifice which God requires,
and with the restatement of the theme in the sixty-ninth
Psalm:

" Hear, O my people, and I will speak . . . I am God, thy
God . . . I will take no bullock out of thy house nor he-goats
out of thy folds; for every beast of the forest is mine and the
cattle on a thousand hills; I know all the fowls of the mountains; and the wild beasts of the field are mine. If I were
hungry, I would not tell thee: for the world is mine and
the fulness thereof. Will I eat the flesh of bulls or drink the
blood of goats? Offer unto God thanksgiving; and pay thy
vows unto the Most High: and call upon me in the day of
trouble and I will deliver thee, and thou shalt glorify me."
And, in epitome, " I will praise the name of God with a song
and will magnify Him with thanksgiving. This also shall
please the Lord better than an ox or bullock that hath horns
and hoofs. The humble shall see this and be glad; and your
heart shall live that seek God."

In the same way, the ' living and true God ' with which
the prayer ends refers directly to St. Paul's letter to the
Thessalonians in which he reminds them " how ye turned to
God from idols to serve the living and true God; and to
wait for His Son from heaven, whom He raised from the
dead, even Jesus, which delivered us from the wrath to come."

Thus the offering of " this sacrifice of praise for themselves,
their families and friends; for the redemption of their souls,
for the hope of their security and salvation and for which they

now pay their vows to Thee, the eternal, living and true God " would evoke for the early Christians—as it would for us had we their knowledge and devotion—the picture of the Holy Sacrifice about to be offered as fulfilling the search for truth by both Jew and Gentile. And the definition of the Church is still further widened by the reminder that in history the Chosen People were given by revelation the types and shadows of the truth fully to be shown in Christ, while even the strange sacrificial cults and idols of the Gentiles were, in God's providence, capable of leading also to Him.

THE COMMUNICANTES

Joining in communion with and venerating the memory in the first place of the glorious and ever-virgin Mary, Mother of our God and Lord Jesus Christ; as also of Thy blessed apostles and martyrs, Peter and Paul, Andrew, James, John, Thomas, Philip, Bartholomew, Matthew, Simon and Thaddeus (Jude); Linus, Cletus, Clement, Sixtus, Cornelius, Cyprian, Lawrence, Chrysogonus, John and Paul, Cosmas and Damian, and of all Thy saints, by whose merits and prayers grant that we may be defended by the help of Thy protection, through the same Christ our Lord, Amen.

Communicantes et memoriam venerantes, in primis gloriosae semper Virginis Mariae, Genetricis Dei et Domini nostri Jesu Christi: sed et beatorum Apostolorum ac Martyrum tuorum, Petri et Pauli, Andreae, Jacobi, Philippi, Bartolomaei, Matthaei, Simonis et Thaddaei, Leni, Cleti, Clementis, Xysti, Corneli, Cypriani, Laurentii, Chrysogoni, Joannis et Pauli, Cosmae et Damiani, et omnium Sanctorum tuorum; quorum meritis precibusque concedas, ut in omnibus protectionis tuae muniamur auxilio. Per eumdem Christum Dominum nostrum. Amen.

THE CHURCH is not only the Church Militant. The greater part of it is the Church Triumphant. " The Church is one in Heaven and on earth. The stern of the vessel no doubt is still in darkness. But the prow advances, shining into the living light of eternal glory. Our stammerings are amplified

54

by the praise of the Saints." In this prayer we call them in to worship with us and though the list inevitably reflects, in some of its choices, the devotional mind of sixth-century Rome rather than that of our own time, yet the more one meditates on it, the less ' archaic ' it becomes. It is not merely that ' and all Thy Saints ' allows us to add—as we should —our own particular saint or patron. It is that, as we study the lives of the saints mentioned here, they seem to embrace all types of sanctity and all kinds of men. Fisherman and tax-collector, mystic and organiser, priest and layman, Jew and Gentile, descendant of the proudest aristocracy of Rome and a humble unknown Greek, lawyer and civil servant and doctor, Pope and zealot—all are here, with others of different temperaments and skills and gifts, ' joining in communion ' with us, so like and so unlike them, on earth.

(i) Our Lady

At the head of the company in heaven stands, necessarily, the mother of Jesus. The simple description in the prayer may seem almost bare in comparison with the wealth of devotional names with which she was to be clothed. Within the five hundred years between St. Augustine of Canterbury and William Rufus, she was to be hailed as ' Star of the Deep and Portal of the Sky ' (in the *Alma Redemptoris*) and ' Holy Queen, Mother of Mercy, our life, our sweetness and our hope ' (in the *Salve Regina*). Such devotion, increasing through the centuries, was to demand in the nineteenth the dogmatic definition of the Immaculate Conception and of the Glorious Assumption in the twentieth. Yet in the quietness of the 'Ever-Virgin Mary, Mother of our God and Lord Jesus Christ' everything else is implicit. The most extravagant-sounding devotion is not, indeed, an over-statement, for to honour her Son is necessarily to honour her—" Shall we not love thee, Mother dear, whom Jesus loves so well?"—and the dogmas defining her status are concerned primarily with his. Not the least of the glories of Mary is that she cannot escape, even if she would, from her humility. And those dogmas are perhaps best understood by seeing them as an extension of that protection she once gave Him in Bethlehem and Nazareth, as well as a vindication of his righteousness who, in glory, could not fail to recompense his mother for the suffering of her sword-pierced heart.

Here, in the single mention of Mary in the Canon, one's thought, so occupied for the most part with her Son's sacrificial and atoning death, dwells specifically on the Incarnation which was made possible, in that way and at that time, by her will. When Gabriel, the envoy of the power of God, saluted her, a girl of sixteen, as blessed among women, she was faced with a choice. She was free to refuse if she so wished to abandon herself to the overshadowing of the Spirit of God which was to initiate the second creation.

The very imagery of the angel's speech, in recalling the creation of the world when the spirit of God brooded over the waters, bringing life where there was no life, emphasised the momentousness of the occasion. Then God had made the world and seen that it was good; but the men, whom He had made in his image, had spoilt it. They had used the freedom of will He had given them to disobey Him and hurt themselves. The power of choice that was theirs they had used to choose the worse instead of the better and to bring upon the world—as they still do in ' the world '—that chain of evil consequences which all bad acts set in motion. But God, still loving them in spite of their desertion, had determined " to renew His image in mankind " by coming to it in his own person. He, who is love, would come to seek and to save that which was lost. But his offer could not be imposed. Had it been, free-will would have been mere make-believe. To the divine initiative someone—some quite ordinary human person—had to say ' Yes.'

Mary, it must be insisted, could have said ' No.' But her answer was: " Be it unto me according to Thy word." And so, in due time, she came to Bethlehem and a stable where a child was born and some shepherds and some Wise Men came to see the paradox of paradoxes—" the hands that had made the sun and the stars too small to reach the huge heads of the cattle " that stood around.

The Incarnation—the fleshing of God—was a thing unique. God, who is spirit, with a human body which knew hunger, thirst, pain and death; a personality which could experience anger and sadness, fear and love; a god who saw things through human eyes, emptying himself of his glory; by his omnipotence fettering his omnipotence for a season with mortal limitations—a mystery beyond understanding, though perhaps in a little way understood by remembering how when you love a child and want to comfort it and really give it sympathy, you have to limit your own knowledge and experience to its ignorance and fear. The very idea of the Incarnation was equally without parallel in the world's thought. There are indeed those who insist on affinities with pre-Christian pantheons, who say for example, that the Virgin Birth is the same idea as the miraculous birth of Athene from the head of Zeus and who point to the gods leaving Olympus to wander the earth in the guise of men. It is difficult to suppose that they really think that springing fully grown and fully armed from the head of a man is the same as being born of woman as an ordinary baby; that assuming human form as a temporary disguise to facilitate enormities of self-indulgence is the same as living a man's life of perfect obedience and humility and ending it, for the salvation of the world, in the most agonising of deaths. Those who believe that these are the same—if they do—have all the credulity of the rationalist, whom the joyful reasonableness of Christianity for ever eludes.

Of all the thousand things for which the Incarnation gives us cause for thankfulness, not the least is that reasonableness —that it suddenly makes sense of the world. Until that moment in history, religions and philosophies (except the Judaism which prepared the way for it) had concentrated on the non-physical side of man's existence—what is loosely called the 'spiritual.' The body was something to be used, despised, endured; the dark envelope which enclosed the light—the 'soul,' the 'real' person to be released at death, while the body, finished with (and good riddance!) moulders away to dust. That was—and is—'religion.' And with life it had little connection, except as a manifestation of pessimism and 'wishful thinking.'

To this philosophy came the eternal No of the Incarnation. God, who had made the body, authenticated it in a new way. *He* became flesh; died and suffered in that flesh; rose again in the body and took that body back into the Godhead, promising that our bodies too, when the deformities of sin had gone, should be made like his glorious body. The 'resurrection of the flesh' became the battle-cry of the early Church against the philosophic pagans. It still is. Against the notion of the immortality of the soul, the Church, founded on the Incarnation, proclaimed the resurrection of the body. "If you fall in with those who teach the immortality of the soul," warned Justin Martyr, "you will know that they are *not* Christians."

The point has been well put by G. K. Chesterton. Because of the Incarnation " there really was a new reason for regarding the senses and the sensations of the body with a reverence . . . which no man in the ancient world could have begun to understand. The body was no longer what it was when Plato and the old mystics had left it for dead. It had hung upon a gibbet. It had risen from a tomb. It was no longer possible for the soul to despise the senses, which had been the organs of something that was more than man. Plato might despise the flesh; but God had not despised it . . . ' Seeing is believing' was no longer the platitude of a mere 'idiot' or common individual, as in Plato's world; it was mixed up with real conditions of real belief. Those revolving mirrors that send messages to the brain of man . . . had truly revealed to God Himself the path to Bethany or the light on the high rock of Jerusalem. These ears that resound to common noises had reported also to the secret knowledge of God the noise of the crowd that strewed palms and the crowd that cried for the Crucifixion. After the Incarnation had become the idea that is central in our civilization, it was inevitable that there should be a return to materialism in the sense of the serious value of matter and the making of the body."

All that this revolution in thought means is impossible to comprehend. But at least it starts with something simple. No longer is 'religion' divorced from 'life.' Our ordinary lives, lived in the limitation of the body; our ordinary understanding, attested by the authority of our senses; our full personalities—spirit, soul and *body*—are to be taken into eternity, where we can fulfil all the potentialities which, because of the shortness of time and our cramping circumstance and our lack of opportunities, we cannot realise on earth. God entered into our human life so that we might enter into his divine life; and, in our gratitude for this guarantee of overflowing abundance, how can we limit our praise of the girl in Galilee who, when the undreamt-of offer was made, said 'Yes'?

To protect her name the Church, through the centuries, has had to fight against the pressure of popular heresies which, hankering after the old 'religion,' tried to transform her into a deity. The meaning of the Incarnation could be destroyed if only the Mother of God were to become thought of as a Mother-Goddess. Against 'Mariolatry'—the worship of Mary—the dogmas of the Immaculate Conception (which safeguarded her freedom of will) and the Glorious Assumption (which was an act of her Son's power) were precisely directed. It is not surprising that still the forces of infidelity fight against her. It is noticeable, as Jean Guitton points out in *The Blessed Virgin*, " that the theology of the Blessed Virgin is bound up so closely with the whole of Catholic theology that any inexactness or plain error in the former is an indication of a

serious lapse in the economy of the latter. The idea of this
close relationship was expressed long ago in the saying: ' All
heresies were brought to nothing by Mary.' More modestly,
we may say Mariology is like a microcosm, reflecting the
macrocosm which is the general theology of the Incarnation,
of Grace and of the Church . . . The idea of the virginal conception guaranteed first the human reality of Jesus against the
Docetists, and then the connection of the Gospel with Israel
against the Marcionites." So it is that by the attitude of any
speculation to Our Lady, the Christian nature of it can be
assessed. It is again Chesterton who has put this into short
and memorable form:

> We know the tale: half truth and double treason,
>   Borgia and Torquemada in the throng;
> Bad men who had no right to their right reason,
>   Good men who had good reason to be wrong.
>
> But when that tangled war our fathers waged
>   Stirred against her—then could we hear right well,
> Through roar of men not wrongfully enraged,
>   The little hiss that only comes from hell.

For it is impossible to love Christ without loving Mary or
to pretend to Christianity and withhold reverence from Mary
—" our tainted nature's solitary boast." Such devotion indeed
is the test that tears the Christian mask from the face of atheist
or infidel; for every baptized Christian can unite in this simple
ascription of the early Church, " Ever-Virgin Mary, Mother
of our God and Lord Jesus Christ," which contains all that
there is.

(ii) *The Apostles*

Following Our Lady come the twelve Apostles, with Paul of Tarsus substituted for Judas Iscariot. Peter stands at the head, with Paul immediately after him. They are always so brought together by the Church. No feast of one is celebrated without a commemoration of the other. Traditionally they were both martyred in Rome under Nero; historically, they are the twin founders of the Church—the ' rock ' to whom Jesus entrusted the keys of the kingdom and the Apostle of the Gentiles, whose crossing into Macedonia was a decisive moment in world-history, ensuring that the gospel came westward to give birth to christendom. So it is natural, one might say, that they should not be separated.

Yet the deeper reason for their closeness is their human opposition. Paul was one of the architects of Europe in defiance of Peter's Palestinian policy; he publicly ' withstood Peter to his face,' and no two human temperaments and gifts,—the simple fisherman with his streak of cowardice, the subtle intellectual with physical courage bordering on bravado; no two experiences of Christ,—the daily contact with the Galilean friend and teacher, the sudden blinding revelation of the Risen Lord; no two expositions of the same eternal truth could differ more widely than those of Peter and Paul. Yet, each bound to Christ, this natural divergence was raised to a supernatural unity. And it is this unity, the dominating *motif* of the whole prayer, which is epitomised in ' Peter and Paul ' and extending by mention of the other ten.

Of the rest, several have their own primacies. Andrew,

Peter's brother, who, when John the Baptist was preaching and baptising by the Jordan, led the others to Jesus is known, on that account, as 'the first disciple' and his feast is always the first of the Christian year. Of the brothers James and John, the 'sons of thunder' who would call down fire from heaven on their master's enemies, James was the first apostle to suffer martyrdom and John, with the unsurpassed title of 'the disciple whom Jesus loved' alone of them dared to stand with Our Lady at the foot of the Cross. Thomas, the doubter, claiming the right of scepticism to demand an answer, (provided that with the questioning goes the humility of mind that will accept the answer and not the arrogance that immediately tries to discover a new difficulty) is given a unique satisfaction. John was never troubled with Thomas's scruples, yet who shall say that, even in the certainty of his love, he had a more profound vision than that which informed Thomas's "My Lord and my God!"?

James and Philip, in proximity here, are so kept by the Church, sharing the feast which displaced the pagan May Day. James, known as 'the less' (because of his stature, not his status) to distinguish him from John's brother, was a relative of Jesus Himself and, on that account, was made first bishop of Jerusalem and presided over the first Council of the Church. A somewhat shadowy figure, dwarfed in our eyes by greater names, James may be seen as the patron of those who, by reason of their birth, are called to public office and who endeavour faithfully to fulfil responsibilities they have not sought and would gladly relinquish.

Philip's destiny was not altogether dissimilar, for, so the tradition of the Church affirms, he was the first of the twelve to become Jesus's constant companion. Though he was called to his discipleship the day after Peter and Andrew, whose fellow-townsman he was, they for a time went back to their fishing-trade. But Philip, from that moment, stayed with Jesus and this obscure fidelity gives an overtone to that moment at the last supper when to Philip's request: " Lord, show us the Father and it sufficeth us! " Jesus answered: " Have I been so long time with you and yet hast thou not known me, Philip? "

Bartholomew and Matthew provide a contrast as violent as any in the list of saints—Nathanael BarTholmai, an ' Israelite in whom there is no guile,' mystic and scholar; and Matthew, the hard-headed tax-collector, the servant of the occupying power of Rome, despised by his Roman masters and hated by his fellow-Jews, the unpardonable ' publican.'

Last and, like Philip and James, linked by a double feast, come Simon the Zealot and Jude (Thaddeus), brother of James the Less. With Simon, political fanaticism intrudes itself. Of the Zealots, the militant patriots, Josephus gives a long account, bewailing the mischief they caused. They were " continually instigating the people to cast off the Roman yoke and assert their native liberty; many of their prime nobility they assassinated as betrayers of their country to a foreign power, openly glorying that they themselves were the benefactors and saviours of it. They abrogated the succession of ancient families and thrust obscure and base-born persons into the priests' office, so that they might oblige the most infamous villains to their party. In short, they stuck at nothing, however horrid or impious."

Of Jude, except his blood relationship to Jesus, nothing is

known but his question at the Last Supper: " Lord, how is it that thou wilt manifest thyself to us and not to the world? " to be given the answer that love, not power, is the key: " If any man love me, he will keep my words; and my Father will love him and we will come unto him and make our abode with him." This, which contains the answer to the Zealots, as to all political Utopias and imposed pacifications, becomes more relevant if Jude was—as many have supposed —also of Simon's party.

Still as part of his answer to Jude, a few sentences later, Jesus said: " Peace I leave with you, my peace I give unto you; not as the world giveth give I unto you. Let not your heart be troubled, neither let it be afraid "; and it is in that moment we may best at this moment, as we approach the re-enactment of the Supper, see the eleven. (The other Judas had left them, some time before, on his own business.)

Eleven young men, the eldest probably not more than thirty, the youngest, John, about sixteen, comprehending little of what they heard, contending even at that meal as to which should be most important in the Kingdom, knew themselves to be at the edge of some great critical event. At least they understood, even if they might find difficult to fulfil, the over-riding command to love one another to the death and were secure in this promise of peace. Yet every one of them, except John, was to die a violent and tortured death. The peace was, indeed, " not as the world giveth "; and through the fire of love which fused their antagonisms, they passed into an indestructible unity.

(iii) Linus, Cletus, Clement

The apostles are followed by Peter's first three successors at Rome, Linus, Cletus (or Anacletus) and Clement. Of the first two, little is known but their names, their status and their martyrdom. As Duchesne says, " we are far from the days when the years, months and days of the Pontifical Catalogue can be given with any degree of exactness. But is it necessary to be exact about Popes of whom we know so little? " The one positive record we have of Anacletus is that he ordained a number of priests. He is also credited with having decreed that all bishops should be consecrated by at least three bishops and that all clerics at their ordination should receive Holy Communion—rules observed everywhere to this day. Between them, Linus and Cletus seem to have governed the Church for about twenty-four years after Peter's martyrdom in A.D. 66.[1]

With their successor, Clement, we are on surer ground. Though his actual identity is still disputed—some holding him to be Paul's fellow-worker at Philippi who is mentioned in the apostle's letter to the church there; others believing him the consul Clemens, cousin to Emperor Domitian— there is no doubt that he is the author of the *Epistle to the Corinthians*, written in the autumn of A.D. 96 at the end of the Domitian persecution. This *Epistle*, one of the most

[1] The oldest known list of the Popes was compiled about A.D. 160, that is to say, within sixty years of the death of the last of the Apostles, John, who outlived these first three successors of Peter. There were then thousands alive who had known the Apostles and their friends and it was, of course, in the high civilisation of Rome, as easy to trace and establish such a line as it would be to-day to verify events of 1894.

precious documents of the early Church, contains the first Christian account of how Mass was said and it establishes that, at least within sixty years of the Last Supper (and, of course, since there was not likely to be any innovation here, from the very beginning), it was an ordered liturgical service, not at a supper-table but at an altar.

"Unto the high-priest (the celebrant-bishop)," writes Clement, "his special 'liturgies' have been appointed, and to the priests their special place is assigned, and on the Levites (deacons) their special 'deaconings' are imposed; the layman is bound by the ordinances for the laity. Let each of you, brethren, make eucharist to God according to his own order, keeping a good conscience and not transgressing the appointed rule of his 'liturgy.'"

This insistence on due order is a distinguishing mark of Clement's thought ("The Apostles received the Gospel for us from the Lord Jesus Christ; Jesus Christ was sent from God. So then Christ is from God and the Apostles from Christ. Both therefore came in due order by the will of God") and it is not out of place to see in these first three successors of a Jewish fisherman a reminder that the ancient Roman virtues of organisation and discipline came early to serve and safeguard the universal Church.

(iv) Sixtus, Cornelius, Cyprian, Laurence

The Roman insistence on due order dictates (even a little pedantically, one may be permitted to think) the next four names. As Sixtus and Cornelius were popes, Cyprian a bishop and Laurence a deacon, ecclesiastical precedence separates

Sixtus from his inseparable deacon, and puts the lesser Cornelius before the greater Cyprian. In our thoughts, however, Sixtus and Laurence are inevitably together.

The Valerian persecution, in which these martyrs perished, is now only a name in a history book; but without some knowledge of it the meaning of their martyrdom is lost. For, from the human point of view, no persecution has been so well justified. Rome, the guardian of civilisation, was at bay. Both frontiers were threatened, the population was decimated with disease, the treasury was empty. " The whole Empire was girt as with an ever-contracting ring of fire. No worse time of misery has ever hemmed in civilisation. The barbarian might at any moment be anywhere and the plague was everywhere."

Ruling the empire was one of its finest men, Valerian, whose household was so full of Christians that it resembled a church. But the political needs of the times were over-riding.

As Archbishop Benson put it in his life of Cyprian, " the essence of the Empire was unity. One army, one law, one senate. The adoration of the majesty of the Emperor, with which no national or local worship interfered, was a necessity which grew more vital as the danger from without grew universal. The most tolerant of emperors could not deny that in the midst of all there was an ever-multiplying power, which defied the central unity. Another unity was growing up and growing everywhere which, as it would not adore Caesar, could not, men thought, but make common cause with the violators from without." So, in 257, on the eve of Valerian's departure at the head of his army to defend the Eastern frontier, he issued an edict by which all bishops and priests were to conform to emperor-worship or be banished, while Christian worship and the use of cemeteries were forbidden on pain of death. The following year saw a second and sterner edict. All bishops, priests and deacons were to be summarily executed; Christian laymen to be banished and their estates confiscated.

Sixtus II became Pope a short time after the first edict and was martyred, less than a year later, a few days after the proclamation of the second. He was celebrating Mass in one of the lesser-known cemeteries off the Appian Way and, while delivering the sermon from his chair, was suddenly arrested. A band of soldiers surrounded him and he was " led away to offer sacrifice to the gods." Refusing, he was brought back and slain there at the altar, with two of his deacons, Felicissimus and Agapitus (who are celebrated with him on the anniversary of that day, August 6, the feast of the Transfiguration).

As he was being prepared for death, his principal deacon, Laurence, said " Why do you abandon me, Father, you who never offer the Holy Sacrifice without your deacon? "

" You will follow me," Sixtus replied, " in three days."

The authorities had a reason for temporarily sparing Laurence, for this gifted and powerful young man, a Spaniard by birth, was known to be the ' brains ' of the Christian community in Rome. To him the Prefect of Rome could speak reasonably, as man to man. After all, what was this emperor-worship but the mere sign of that civic patriotism which, as Roman citizens, they all felt, especially in such a time of crisis? No intelligent man actually worshipped the Emperor, of course, but one had to go through the motions for the sake

of morale. Yet, in Laurence's case, even that might be waived
if he were scrupulous about it, if only the Christians would
make a good contribution to the Treasury. Rome was at war
for its life. Rome had afforded the Christians—as well as
those of other faiths, for Rome was essentially tolerant—
safety to practise their religion. Everyone knew that the
Christians had valuable treasures—gold chalices, silver candle-
sticks, jewelled vestments. To ask for these was only to ask
of the Church that help which, at such an hour, all men of
good will were only too pleased to give the State; and if they
were surrendered, the Prefect would be prepared to turn a
blind eye to Christian worship, edict or no edict. Laurence
would understand the necessities of politics, economic
pressure. . . .

The argument is modern enough—and timeless; nor is
there reason to suppose that Laurence had overlooked the
connection between the crisis, the edict and the empty
Treasury. He seemed impressed by the Prefect's reasoning,
did not deny the Church's possession of wealth but said that
it would take time to assemble it. Might he have three days?
The Prefect, delighted by the impression he had made,
readily agreed.

Laurence, realising that eventually the possessions of the
Church would be discovered and confiscated, used the time
to sell them and distribute the money to the Christian poor.
Then, on the appointed day, he took the Prefect to the building
in which he had promised to assemble the treasures of the
Church and, throwing the doors open, pointed to a crowd of
the poor and outcast, the blind, the lame and the diseased.
"These," he said, "are the treasures of the Church, both

because of their inestimable gift of faith and because they convert our alms into imperishable treasures for us."

The Prefect, beside himself with mortification and fury, ordered Laurence to be executed at once by the most painful method he could imagine—a slow roasting to death on a huge gridiron.

For us in the mid-twentieth century—this 'century of martyrs'—Sixtus and Laurence have a relevance which largely eluded our forebears in the nineteenth; and no one, daily praying the Mass and remembering their names here, is ever likely to mistake the rights and wrongs of any persecution of the 'intolerant' Church by a 'reasonable' State.

Of Valerian's fate, nothing is known. He was taken prisoner by the Persians and disappears from history. But, in popular remembrance, Laurence's gridiron is shored against oblivion and a representation (though not, of course, an authentic portrait) of Sixtus, has its place in one of the most famous pictures in the world—for the pope of less than a year whose own blood was shed at the altar is he who kneels rapt in timeless adoration in Raphael's 'Sistine Madonna.'

Cyprian, bishop of Carthage, receiving in Africa the news of Valerian's policy, knew that he, too, was marked to die. But—it was characteristic of him—he determined to choose his own time and place. His 'confession' should not be made in a corner. So, until the proconsul Galerius came in person from Rome to Carthage to try him, he would not be found. From his hidden retreat, he wrote to his clergy explaining that " the city in which he presides over the Church of the Lord is the place in which a Bishop ought to confess his Lord."

On Galerius's arrival, Cyprian immediately returned to his

own house in Carthage and was at once arrested. The proconsul agreed with the bishop and was determined that his killing should for example's sake be as public as possible— for Cyprian, the famous lawyer who, at the age of forty, had turned Christian, was, for Christian and non-Christian alike, the leading figure, certainly in Carthage, perhaps in Africa.

" You are Thascius Cyprianus? " the Proconsul asked.

" I am."

" You have allowed yourself to become a pontiff for those of sacrilegious views."

" I have."

" The most Sacred Emperors have ordered you to sacrifice."

" I shall not."

" You should think of yourself."

" Do what is commanded of you. The matter is too obvious for there to be anything to consider."

" Your life," said Galerius, " has long been led in a sacrilegious mode of thought; you have associated yourself with a very large number of persons in criminal complicity; you have constituted yourself an antagonist to the gods of Rome and to their sacred observances. Nor have our most pious and hallowed princes, and Valerian the most noble Caesar, been able to recall you to the obedience of their own ceremonial. And therefore, as you have been clearly detected as the instigator and standard-bearer in heinous offences, you shall in your own person be a lesson to those you have by your guilt associated with you. Discipline shall be ratified in your blood." Then, taking the prepared tablets, he read: " Our pleasure is that Thascius Cyprianus be executed with the sword."

" Thanks be to God," answered Cyprian.

Immediately the Christian multitude raised the cry: "Let us, too, be beheaded with him" and there was the beginning of a disturbance. Cyprian, guarded by a detachment of the famous Third Legion, was hurried to the place of execution, a level space surrounded by wooded slopes. To this natural amphitheatre, all Carthage came to see him die. The Christians, standing near him, strewed the grass with linen cloths to keep as relics stained with his blood. From one of these, Cyprian took a handkerchief and bound it over his eyes. With his accustomed largesse, he ordered his executioner to be given twenty-five gold pieces. He spoke no more; for he had already defined in one sentence the eternal issue between Christ and Caesar: "The matter is too obvious for there to be anything to consider." And when, at one stroke his head was severed, the pagan citizens of Carthage pressed nearer to gaze on the man who had been the acknowledged benefactor of their city, but who would sooner die than consider whether he could worship the civic gods.

Hardly less important than Cyprian's final witness for the Church was his work within it. The times demanded exactly his cool, incisive brain, his literary ability, his gift of persuasive oratory and his commanding position as bulwarks against the flood of emotionalism released by the circumstances of the persecution.

When, in 249, the assault on Christianity started, it fell on a Church which a period of peace had unfitted to meet it. Multitudes rushed to the Capitol to sacrifice, amid the mockery of the heathen. Others bought certificates of sacrifice which served as exemption. Many of the clergy fled into hiding. Those who stood firm, the 'confessors' and martyrs became, in consequence, so venerated that, when the persecution slackened, they were popularly allowed what amounted to a power of absolution. If, from one of them, the lapsed could obtain *libelli* restoring them to the communion from which, by their apostasy, they had cut themselves off, the local churches in most cases accepted them.

The human situation is the more comprehensible to us, in that something like it occurred in occupied countries during the war. The ' resistance leader ' whose nerves and temperament enabled him to dare and endure suffering better than his frail and timid fellow gained a kudos which, in the popular mind, gave him an absolute superiority. But because he stayed when the administrator ran, it did not follow that, in the conditions of peace, he could take the administrator's place. Even more certainly, because a brave layman ' witnessed ' while a cowardly priest hid, the former was not therefore entitled by his courage to claim the priestly privilege of absolution any more than the latter, by his cowardice, lost it.

Thus Cyprian, on the one hand had to assert this truth in the teeth of popular opinion—to insist that the immediate reconciliation of a ' lapsed ' on the word of a ' confessor ' was not possible. On the other hand, he had to maintain, against the powerful rigorist party in the Church, that the ' lapsed,' after proper penance, *could* be reconciled. This was the greater danger since this ' puritan ' party—the Novatianist schism, " which deepened its unforgivingness at last to heresy " —was exceptionally strong at Rome.

There Cornelius, the patrician Pope descended from Sulla,[1]

[1] " He was a Roman of the Romans. Apart even from the other Popes with their Greek epigraphs, he was buried under a Latin inscription among the noble Cornelia."—Benson: *Cyprian.*

stood against the rising flood. Though the rigorist Novatian made himself anti-Pope, Cornelius supported Cyprian's proposals to reserve the cases of the Lapsed intact, whether the martyrs had given them letters of peace or not, until Councils of the bishops assembling both at Rome and Carthage should lay down some general principles. Meanwhile to mercy and the martyrs, this much was conceded,—any lapsed person in danger of death who had a letter might be readmitted to communion by the imposition of the hands of any priest (or, in desperate cases, of any deacon).

So Cornelius, in his short pontificate, rallied the Church and, with Cyprian (who also wrote his great treatise *On the Unity of the Church*) saved its unity.

At the renewal of the persecution in 253, Cornelius was sent into exile and, within six months, died of the rigours of it, for which reason he is reckoned among the martyrs. Cyprian, writing to congratulate him on the glory of his 'confession' said: "If either of us, prevented by God's mercy, should precede the other in death, may our friendship continue in the Lord and our prayer to the merciful Father for our brethren and sisters never cease."

And though they died different deaths at different times, the Church has refused to separate them but observes the feast of "Ss. Cornelius and Cyprian" on the day of Cyprian's martyrdom and joins them, a unity living and dying for unity, here in the Canon.

(v) *Chrysogonus, John and Paul, Cosmas and Damian*

Of Chrysogonus nothing is known except that he was a

Greek by birth and suffered in the Diocletian persecution at the end of the third century. With him, the East comes into the unity—a thought which is emphasised by the memorial of Cosmas and Damian, brothers born in Arabia and practising as physicians in the seaport of Aegea (now Ayash) on the gulf of Iskanderun.

Because Cosmas and Damian refused to accept payment for their services, regarding their gift of healing as a trust from Christ, they were nicknamed Anangyroi, the ' silverless ones '; and it is not fanciful to see a deliberate and intended connection with St. Peter's words to the lame man at the beautiful gate: " Silver and gold have I none, but such as I have I give thee: in the name of Jesus Christ of Nazareth, rise up and walk."

The brothers were martyred in 287—in the same persecution as Chrysogonus—and were buried at the city of Cyrus in Syria. Two hundred and fifty years later, Justinian I restored the city in their honour and at the same time a church dedicated to them was built in Rome. That was only about sixty years before Augustine came to England and its famous mosaics, ' modern ' to him, are still among the art treasures of the world. Though to-day we cannot perhaps give to the names ' Cosmas and Damian ' the overtones they must have had for him when he first said this prayer at Canterbury, yet the Christ of those mosaics can still be seen no farther away than Hampton Court—for from them Raphael, when he designed the tapestries whose original cartoons now hang there, copied, almost exactly, the face of his Christ.

Last in time, though not in order, come the brothers John and Paul, two officials of the imperial court which, having gone officially Christian under Constantine the Great, went with the flexible facility of courts, back to heathenism as soon as Julian the Apostate made it fashionable. John and Paul, however, were honest men and their failure to apostasize led to their execution in their own house on the Caelian Hill about 363. Within twenty years this house, with their tombs in it, became a Christian church and it is still one of the most important early Christian memorials in Rome.

So, with four laymen—two Christian civil servants and two christian doctors—ends the first list of saints in the Canon, historically precise, yet symbolically timeless, and giving us leave, in the ' and all Thy saints,' to call on others of our own particular choice from the great multitude of witnesses who, since 597, have trodden the same road in the same Faith and are at one with us in the same Mass.

Note to Communicantes

On each of the five great feasts of Jesus in history—his birth, his showing to the world when the wise kings came to do homage to Him, his Resurrection, his Ascension and his sending of the Holy Spirit[1]—there is inserted into the Communicantes a short, special memorial of the day. They are as follows:

Christmas: " In communion with, and celebrating the most sacred day (or, at midnight Mass, ' night ') when the inviolate virginity of Blessed Mary gave forth to this world a Saviour . . ."

No Mass, of course, is ever said on Good Friday.

77

Epiphany: " In communion with, and celebrating the most
sacred day, whereon Thine only-begotten Son,
co-eternal with Thee in Thy glory, was mani-
fested visibly and corporeally in the reality of
our flesh . . ."

Easter: " In communion with, and celebrating the most
sacred day of the Resurrection of our Lord
Jesus Christ, according to the flesh . . ."

Ascension: " In communion with, and celebrating the most
sacred day whereon our Lord, Thine only-
begotten Son, sat down at the right-hand of
Thy glory, the substance of our frailty united
to Himself . . ."

Pentecost: " In communion with, and celebrating the most
sacred day of Pentecost, whereon the Holy
Spirit appeared to the Apostles in innumerable
tongues . . "

THE HANC IGITUR

We therefore beseech Thee, O Lord, graciously to accept this offering which we, Thy servants, and Thy whole family make unto Thee; and to order our days in Thy peace and to deliver us from eternal damnation and to number us in the flock of Thine elect. Through Christ our Lord. Amen.

Hanc igitur oblationem servitutis nostrae, sed et cunctae familiae tuae, quaesumus, Domine, ut placatus accipias: diesque nostros in tua pace disponas, atque ab aeterna damnatione nos eripi, et in electorum tuorum jubeas grege numerari. Per Christum Dominum nostrum. Amen.

(i) *Family and Flock*

THE PRECISE definition of the Church is in this short prayer epitomised in the two simple words, 'family' and 'flock.' For the Church throughout the whole world, with its chief bishop and its bishops, with our friends and our fellow-worshippers, with Christ's mother and his apostles, with the saints and with the martyrs, is, when all is said, a family whose members, however different, share the same home and heritage. We are ' of the race of God '—as St. Paul reminded the Athenians that even their own poets had understood. And " since we compose God's family, as the prayer affirms, we really belong to it, one family with Him in the

79

invisible home of His Spirit" is Zundel's comment on the words. "We could not be more ennobled."

Yet the metaphor of the family seems almost a 'modern' and even an 'intellectual' concept by comparison with that of the flock. In an urbanised civilisation and a technological world, the shepherd-life of the East can still evoke overwhelming associations which might be described as the paradox of a nostalgia for something never known. Even those who would consider themselves liberated from Christianity seldom dispense with the twenty-third Psalm. So the Church is most vividly realised as the flock of the good Shepherd, Whose voice it knows and who has given his life for it that He may lead it in safety through the valley of the shadow of death.

The specific reference in the prayer, 'the flock of Thine elect,' pointed by the petition to be delivered from eternal damnation, is, of course, to the parable of the sheep and the goats: "When the Son of Man shall come in his glory, and all the holy angels with him, then shall he sit upon the throne of his glory and before him shall be gathered all nations: and he shall separate one from another, as a shepherd divideth his sheep from the goats: and he shall set the sheep on his right hand, but the goats on the left. Then shall the King say unto them on his right hand, Come ye blessed of my Father, inherit the kingdom prepared for you from the foundation of the world: for I was an hungred and ye gave me meat: I was thirsty and ye gave me drink: I was a stranger and ye took me in: naked and ye clothed me: I was sick and ye visited me: I was in prison and ye came unto me. Then shall the righteous answer him saying, Lord, when saw we thee an hungred and fed thee? or thirsty and gave thee drink?

when saw we thee a stranger and took thee in? or naked and clothed thee? or when saw we thee sick or in prison and came unto thee? And the King shall answer and say unto them, Verily I say unto you, Inasmuch as ye have done it unto one of the least of these my brethren, ye have done it unto me."

The entire context here is of importance—the reason for the division as well as the division itself—for there are few passages in Scripture which, by convicting us of our failure to deserve it, so reinforce the necessity of our plea for acceptance, which is the core of the prayer. As Father Martindale has pointedly expressed it, " you would say that the priest . . . lets everything go on one side save the vast thoughts of eternal loss, eternal salvation, and in an all-but clumsy, roughened style, drops everything save this almost grim petition to his God."

And behind the parable are the older associations of mercy and promise which the very mention of the ' flock ' recalls—not only the psalmist's picture but the great passages of the prophets, which the fathers knew so well—Isaiah's foretelling of Messias who " shall feed his flock like a shepherd; he shall gather the lambs with his arms and carry them in his bosom and shall gently lead those that are with young "; and Jeremiah's promise that " he that scattered Israel will gather him and keep him as a shepherd doth his flock," and the culminating paean of Ezekiel: " Thus saith the Lord God: Behold I, even I, will both search my sheep and seek them out. As a shepherd seeketh out his flock in the day that he is among his sheep that are scattered, so will I seek out my sheep and will deliver them out of all the places where they have been scattered in the cloudy and dark day . . . and I will feed them in a good pasture and upon the high mountains of Israel shall their fold be."

(ii) *The Dedication of the Victim*

The pastoral life of the East supplies more than the symbolism of the shepherd and the flock; it gives us, too, the lamb of sacrifice. And the *Hanc Igitur* is specifically the prayer of the dedication of the victim. The priest, as he says it, stretches out his hands over the oblations of bread and wine in the same manner as the Jewish priest laid his hands on the sacrificial offering to indicate that it was a substitute for himself and for those who had provided it. "Thou shalt take a ram and Aaron and his sons shall put their hands upon the head of the ram and thou shalt slay the ram and thou shalt take his blood . . ."—so run the instructions for sacrifice under the old covenant. In this action under the New Covenant, a bell is rung to let all the congregation know that *they*, represented by the oblation they have provided, are being offered. It is here, at this precise point, that (in the words of one of the prayers in the Book of Common Prayer) "we offer and present unto Thee, O Lord, ourselves, our souls and bodies, to be a reasonable, holy and lively sacrifice." We are about to be presented with Him, so that we may truly say:

> Look, Father, look on His anointed face
> And only look on us as found in Him.

The bell is rung so that those who cannot actually see the

priest's action shall know the moment—and associate themselves in prayer with it—when they are formally dedicated on the altar. In the simplicity of that ritual action, the whole theology of the Atonement is expressed. Sinful man lays himself on the altar, ready to be immolated in expiation of his sins; but the only offering which can achieve atonement is the God-Man. "The offering," says Dom Eugène Vandeur with exactitude, "represents on the one hand, the faithful, on the other, Christ . . . The priest, acting for himself and for the people whom he represents, lays his hands upon the chalice and the host, as though upon the head of Jesus Christ, Who invites us to load Him with our faults and to recognize that He alone can merit for us pardon for our sins."

(iii) "Order our days in Thy peace"

These words—*diesque nostros in tua pace disponas*—were, we are told by our own historian, the venerable Bede, added to the *Hanc Igitur* by Gregory the Great. This human cry from history has, however, no feeling of intrusion, but reinforces poignantly the single-mindedness of this prayer of 'grim petition.'

As the year 590 opened, Rome seemed on the brink of destruction. Not only were the barbarians at the gate and half Italy lost to the Lombards, but nature itself seemed to have turned enemy. Throughout the countryside, unprecedented floods had carried away whole farmsteads. In the city, Tiber had overflowed its banks and destroyed not only public and private buildings but the granaries with their vital supply of corn. To the famine which ensued was added plague in its most terrible form—a Black Death. Men went mad in the streets. Rome became a desert where the only business was the rumble of death-carts piled high with corpses for burial in huge common pits outside the walls. The Pope himself was one of the victims and Gregory, despite his attempts to avoid it, was chosen as his successor.

Preaching to the terrified people, he thundered the Christian truth: " Fiery swords, reddened with the blood of mankind which soon after flowed in streams, were seen in the heavens before Italy became the prey of the Lombards. Be watchful and alert! Those who love God should shout for joy at the end of the world. Those who mourn are they whose hearts are rooted in love for the world and who neither long for the future life nor have any foretaste of it within themselves. Every day the earth is visited by fresh calamities. You see how few remain of the ancient population; each day sees us chastened by new afflictions and unforeseen blows strike us to the ground. The world grows old and hoary and through a sea of troubles hastens to approaching death."

But he was to see, too, in the heavens a sword sheathed. One of his first acts as Pope was to call on the people to go in penetential processions, one from each of the seven districts of Rome and all meeting at the Basilica of the Blessed Virgin, to pray for pardon and the cessation of the pestilence. As he himself, barefooted, was leading the seven-fold procession over the Aelian Bridge, he saw in the clouds over the mausoleum of Hadrian, Michael the Archangel sheathing his sword —and still to-day the name to which the mausoleum was then changed, Sant' Angelo, the Holy Angel, commemorates that moment.

Though Gregory, Roman of the Romans, looking on the scene of temporal destruction, could not forbear from crying: "Where is the Senate? Where are the people? The bones are dissolved; the flesh consumed; all the pomp and dignities of the world are gone," Gregory the Christian could say: "To him who sees the Creator, all creation is small indeed." And it was this contrast, which is also the contrast of his sermon, which is enshrined in the simple words: "Order our days in *Thy* peace" to stand for ever here as a reminder of Christian values among the chances and changes of this mortal world.

The Christian cannot ask for 'peace' in the worldly sense. That, he knows, despite the promises of politicians, is an impossibility. Even if he may live in places and times which are temporarily secure, as Victorian Englishmen lived, his own warfare is often thereby intensified. As one of the greatest of Victorian Englishmen, John Henry Newman, reminded his generation: "What we want is to *understand* that we are in the place in which the early Christians were, with the same covenant, ministry, sacraments, duties; to realize a state of things long passed away; to feel that we are in a sinful world, a world lying in wickedness; to discern our position in it, that we are witnesses in it, that reproach and suffering are our portion, so that we must not 'think it strange' if they come upon us, but a kind of gracious exception if they do not; to have our hearts awake to the hope and waiting of His second coming, looking out for it, nay, desiring to see tokens of it."

And one of the tokens of it we know, from Christ's own words: "Then shall be great tribulation, such as was not from the beginning of the world to this time, no, nor ever shall be; and, except those days should be shortened, there should no flesh be saved."

These terrible days, which are the prelude to judgment, are presupposed in this prayer; and it was surely not without inspiration that Gregory the Great, in a moment which seemed like a rehearsal of them, should have inserted the petition to serve all Christians who might have to live through similar experiences: " Order our days in *Thy* peace."

Note to Hanc Igitur

The *Hanc Igitur*, like the *Communicantes* has, on certain days, additions made to it. The days chosen, Maundy Thursday, Easter and Pentecost were the occasions on which those baptized on the previous evenings made their first communions and Maundy Thursday is the anniversary of Christ's self-dedication in the Blessed Sacrament.

The additions are:

Maundy Thursday: . . . and Thy whole family make unto Thee in memory of the day on which our Lord Jesus Christ gave to His disciples the mysteries of His Body and Blood to be celebrated; and to order our days . . .

Easter and Pentecost: . . . and Thy whole family make unto Thee on behalf of these whom Thou hast vouchsafed to bring to a new birth by water and the Holy Ghost, giving them remission of all their sins: and to order our days . . .

THE QUAM OBLATIONEM

Which oblation do Thou, O God, vouchsafe in all respects to
make blessed, approved, ratified, reasonable and acceptable, that
it may be made for us the Body and Blood of Thy most beloved
Son Jesus Christ our Lord,

Quam oblationem tu Deus in omnibus, quaesumus, benedictam,
adscriptam, ratam, rationabilem acceptabilemque facere digneris;
ut nobis Corpus et Sanguis fiat dilectissimi Filii tui Domini nostri
Jesu Christi,

THIS SHORT prayer is both a summary and a transition. On
the one hand it forms the conclusion to all the preceding
offertory prayers; on the other, it leads from those prayers
to the Institution-narrative which follows immediately. (It
ends with a comma and proceeds ". . . our Lord Jesus Christ,
Who the day before He suffered, took bread . . .") In its
earliest form, in the fourth century, it was a prayer *for* the
Consecration and it is still considered by some writers to be
the *epiclesis* of the Roman rite—that is to say, the invocation
of the Holy Spirit to come upon the elements and transform
them into the Body and the Blood. In the sixth century, on
its revision, the emphasis shifted and the petition is now
rather that our offering may have been duly performed in

87

order that the Transformation may follow. The terms of it have almost a legalistic flavour.

(i) " *In due order* "

The five words used are, indeed, the reflection of the grave Roman mind—*benedictam, adscriptam, ratam, rationabilem, acceptabilem*—and their translation is difficult. *Rationabilem*, 'reasonable' recalls at once St. Paul's: "I beseech you, brethren, that ye present your bodies a living sacrifice, holy, acceptable unto God, which is your reasonable service" and this allusiveness, like other examples in the liturgy, is intentional. The Pauline precept, indeed, sums up our prayer of self-offering. But the word here means both more and less —more, because one of the connotations in the Pauline use is 'spiritual,' and therefore the sense can be, as it has been construed, "reasonable, because this oblation will soon be Christ Himself"; less, because "the word as used here has already in the earlier form of the prayer, come to mean 'in due form,' and is surrounded by words of a similarly legal flavour."

Adscriptam, usually translated as 'approved' means in its secular context something like 'entered on the rolls.' 'Enrolled in the Book of Life' would give something of its force, though the simple 'registered,' with its recent everyday associations for a nation at war, is a truer approximation to its matter-of-factness. In the same way, *ratam*, 'ratified' suggests a confirmatory signature or seal and *acceptabilem*, 'acceptable' is a formal acknowledgment.

At first encounter, the words almost repel by their coldness. There is even a danger that at first we may try to 'spiritualise' them or at least to attach to them an emotional construction which they will not bear. Yet the more one knows and uses the Liturgy, the more right they are seen to be. They are, like most Latin prayers "as bare as the old basilicas whose beauty, devoid of apparent mystery, is exposed wholly legible to the glance" and yet yield more to each closer look. Here, as the immediate prelude to the Mystery of Mysteries, we fall back on the conventional language of contractual obedience. For there is no other. We have done —or tried to do—everything in due order. Like Elijah, we have built the altar as we have been instructed. We can do nothing but ask God to authorise it by His signature and wait for Him to send the fire.

(ii) " Nobis "

We pray that the bread and the wine " may be made for us (or unto us) the Body and the Blood "—*ut nobis Corpus et Sanguis fiat.* In the word *nobis* all the unfortunate controversies which, down the ages, have raged about the Table of the Lord are resolved and stilled.

It is well to remind ourselves once more that this prayer reaches back at least to the fourth century. That is to say, it is nine hundred years older than the definition of 'Transubstantiation' in 1215 and it is still said, unchanged, seven hundred years after that definition.

The word 'Transubstantiation' itself is popularly misunderstood, because the strict scholastic definition of 'substance,' in which it depends, is forgotten. The philosophy of the Schoolmen held that we can perceive with our senses only the qualities or 'accidents' of things. Bread, for example, has a certain taste, of which our tongue can inform us; a certain appearance, which we can see with our eyes; a certain texture, which we know by touch; a certain smell. By our senses we can 'recognise' bread. Yet none of these things is the bread itself; they are its 'accidents'; behind them is the 'substance' of the bread in which they cohere. And this 'substance'—which *is* 'bread'—is completely beyond the range of all our senses, including the sense of touch.

We cannot, therefore, see even the bread on the altar; we can only see its 'accidents' and these 'accidents' remain unchanged, even when the 'substance' of the bread is changed into the 'substance' of the Body and Blood of Christ.

As an explanation, in the philosophical terms of the age, of the mode of fulfilment of Christ's words : "This is My Body" and "This is My Blood," this could hardly be improved. Nor can there be any logical disagreement with the definition of the Council of Trent in the sixteenth century: " If anyone shall deny that wonderful and singular conversion of the whole substance of the bread into the Body and of the whole substance of the wine into the Blood, the appearance only of the bread and wine remaining, which conversion indeed the Catholic Church most fittingly calls Transubstantiation, let him be anathema."

The confusion has arisen because of the popular use of the term 'substance' to denote what are, in technical language, the 'accidents.' If a man should say: " I can see with my eyes and taste with my tongue that the substance which I am given is bread " or if he should insist: " I am willing to accept on faith that this is the Body of our Lord, but I must insist that, with it, is the substance of bread " he would be saying something which everyone could understand and with his *meaning* of which every believer in Transubstantiation would agree. He would merely be using, in the context, the wrong words. He would be asserting, in his own language, precisely what the Church asserts: " The change of ' substance ' I accept on faith—for the ' substance ' of anything is imperceptible to the senses; but the ' accidents ' which I can see with my eyes and taste with my tongue are undoubtedly those of bread."

The division of opinion between Christians is not, once this is understood, between those who believe in ' some kind of change in the elements ' and those who call the change ' Transubstantiation '; it is between those who believe in Transubstantiation and those who believe that the bread remains bread and the wine remains wine in what is only a ' memorial meal '; between those who believe that they are receiving the Body and the Blood in a Sacrament and those who believe that their faith is spiritually quickened by eating bread and drinking wine in an act of remembrance.

The cleavage is between what may be called for simplicity's sake the ' mechanical ' view and the ' receptionist ' view. Does the bread and the wine, automatically, so to speak, become the Body and Blood or is the efficacy of the Sacrament dependent on the faith of the recipient? One is tempted to think that, had the *Quam oblationem* been understood fully and *prayed* by the laity, there would have been no schisms; for the alternatives are false.

This matter has been so well put by Zundel, writing as a Roman Catholic priest in a book which has received the *imprimatur,* that quotation will be wiser than an attempt to express it in my own words: " The material offering which we dedicated in all the offertory prayers was clearly but the symbol of the wholly spiritual gift of ourselves which is the essential demand of the sacrifice in which we are taking part. In any event Christ's assent is pledged and His word on the priest's lips will infallibly effect what it states. But though really endowed with His presence, the consecrated Bread and Wine will avail nothing unless our love assimilates them, spiritually making them *for us* what they actually are in themselves, the Body and Blood of our Lord Jesus Christ."

This thought, reconciling opposing ideas, is also present in the invocation of the holy Spirit in the Byzantine liturgies—the epiclesis—though it comes after the Consecration, that the bread and the wine may become *for us*, by the power of the Holy Ghost, our Lord's Body and Blood.

THE QUI PRIDIE

Who, the day before He suffered, took bread into His holy and
adorable hands and, with His eyes raised to Heaven, unto Thee,
God, His Almighty Father, giving thanks to Thee, He blessed,
broke and gave it to His disciples, saying: Take and eat ye all
of this. This is My Body.

In like manner, after supper, taking this precious Chalice into
His Holy and adorable hands, and giving thanks to Thee, He
blessed it and gave to His disciples, saying: Take and drink
ye all of this, for this is the Chalice of My Blood, of the new
and eternal Covenant: the mystery of faith: which shall be
shed for you and for many for the remission of sins.

As often as ye shall do these things, ye shall do them in
remembrance of Me.

Qui pridie quam pateretur, accepit panem in sanctas ac venerabiles
manus suas: et elevatis oculis in caelum ad te, Deum Patrem
suum onmipotentem, tibi gratias agens, benedixit fregit,
deditque discipulis suis, dicens: Accipite et manducate ex hoc
omnes. Hoc est enim Corpus Meus.

Simili modo postquam coenatum est, accipiens et hunc
praeclarum Calicem in sanctas ac venerabiles manus suas: item
tibi gratias agens, benedixit deditque discipulis suis, dicens:
Accipite et bibite ex eo omnes. Hic est enim Calix Sanguinis
mei, novi et aeterni testamenti: mysterium fidei: qui pro vobis
et pro multis effundetur in remissionem peccatorum.

Haec quotienscumque feceritis, in mei memoriam facietis.

(i) *The Institution Narrative*

THE NARRATIVE of the institution of the Eucharist is the core of the Liturgy. During the early centuries, however the Great Prayer might be revised and enlarged, this recital of what Jesus said and did at the Last Supper kept its place at the centre of it. It is the formula of consecration. The priest, acting by virtue of Christ's own eternal priesthood[1] has always repeated the words and performed the actions which, on a particular evening, took place in an Upper Room.

The *Qui Pridie* is basically an older account of the institution of the Eucharist than those contained in the New Testament. By the time that St. Paul wrote down the formula in his first letter to the Church at Corinth, over twenty years after the Resurrection, the Eucharist had been celebrated many thousand times. He, as well as the authors of the Gospels who wrote even later, was repeating what was already established in the Church, and his account, like that of his friend St. Luke, reflects that already in use in the Liturgy. And the difference between their version and that given by St. Matthew and St. Mark—where the words spoken over the chalice immediately follow those spoken over the bread—is itself an indication of a development in the Church's practice.

The paschal meal which Jesus ate with His disciples was a long and elaborate ceremonial. Before the supper itself came the memorial of the escape from Egypt, in which bitter herbs

---

[1] " At this moment more than any other, the principal priest is Jesus Christ. The person of the minister hides from our sight, so to say. He will without doubt consecrate, but the principal priest is Jesus Christ . . . (The celebrant) does these things only by virtue of the inflowing in him of Christ, Priest of His Father." Dom Eugène Vandeur *The Holy Mass.*

and unleavened bread were eaten; wine was drunk; the story of the first Passover was told; and prayer of thanksgiving was said and the first part of the Hallel (Psalms 113 and 114) were sung. The meal proper began when the head of the company took one of the loaves, broke it, pronounced a blessing and passed it round for all to share. This communal partaking of the one bread was the signal for the start of the supper. When it was over and the paschal lamb had been consumed, the head of the company filled a cup with wine and, raising it slightly, said the thanksgiving grace. Then all in turn drank of this ' chalice of benediction ' before the singing of the second part of the Hallel (Psalms 115-118 and 136).

There was thus a long interval between the breaking of the bread and the drinking of the cup, and this interval is preserved in the form of the *Qui Pridie* and in the Pauline and the Lucan accounts. But Matthew and Mark, in making the blessing of the chalice immediately follow the blessing of the bread, reflect what actually happens in the Eucharist, as it is celebrated. For, though instituted in the context of the Passover meal, the Eucharist immediately became a new and independent rite. Apart from anything else, the fact that the Passover was celebrated only once a year made this a necessity.

Into the narrative of the consecration of the wine, some explanatory theological expressions have found their way. The most obvious of these is the exclamation ' the mystery of faith.' Its origin has never been satisfactorily determined. Some have supposed it to be a private devotion of Pope Anicetus, who was responsible for the final form of the

Qui Pridie about A.D. 160; others think the words were originally uttered by the deacon. In the same way, the words ' and eternal ' have been added in description of the New Covenant, as if to point that, though the Old Covenant has passed away, this can never be superseded. It is new, but it can never become old. " Beyond the Christian Gift, nothing remains."

The third phrase to notice is ' *this precious* Chalice ' which differs from all the New Testament accounts. It is as if, at that moment, the identification of every Mass with the Last Supper is insisted on—" in the matter of that Supper, of Calvary and of Mass, time vanishes and the Action is one and the selfsame throughout." This indeed must be the symbolic construction put on the words to-day. It may be for that purpose that the words were inserted into the narrative. And yet could there not be another explanation of them and one which is consonant with the priority of the *Qui Pridie*? Might not, in the beginning, ' this precious Chalice ' have been an exact description of the cup which was used, because in the first Eucharists in Jerusalem, that cup was the very same which had been used in the Upper Room?[1]

(ii) " The day before "

The setting of the Eucharist within the paschal meal has an obvious reference to the past. The Mosaic Law, the terms of a unique covenant between God and his Chosen People, was

[1] This is only a personal opinion and has no authority behind it, but it has always seemed to me the most obvious explanation of the words. The objection that had this been so, the Chalice of the Last Supper would have been preserved as the most precious of relics, is surely met by remembering the sack and destruction of Jerusalem less than forty years later.

now at an end; but from it Jesus took the ritual form for the institution which was to succeed it and so, for the last time, fulfilled the Law without destroying it. On that night in that upper room, the meaning of the Law was summed up in some broken bread and a cup of shared wine. These Jesus took and used for His new and eternal covenant. As St. Thomas Aquinas put it in his great Eucharistic hymn, *Lauda Sion*:

> Lo, the new King's Table gracing
> This new Passover of blessing
> Hath fulfilled the elder rite:
> Now the new the old effaceth,
> Truth revealed the shadow chaseth,
> Day is breaking on the night.

Yet even more important for us is the relationship of the Last Supper to what was to come after—to Calvary. For without the one, the other is merely a miscarriage of justice, a sordid end to a shameful trial. It is the Last Supper which makes Calvary sacrificial. It was not the Crucifixion in itself, but the Crucifixion as the Last Supper interpreted it, which constitutes Christ's sacrifice. In the Upper Room on Thursday, He, as priest, offered Himself as victim. On the Cross of Friday He made the sacrifice in his Body and Blood. At the Supper, the offering was made under the form of bread and wine in the context of a recognised sacrificial meal. By a consecratory action, sacramentally separating the body from the blood, Jesus prefigured the actual death which next day would take place on a cross on a hill in the context of a public execution—the one, unrepeatable Offering which was to obtain eternal redemption for mankind.

" Giving Himself wholly," writes Dom Eugène Masure in *The Christian Sacrifice*, " He gives Himself only once, but in two ways, one ritual, one historic and both real. The unity of the victim is absolute, so that the two sacrifices, one within the other, despite the external differences which permit us to distinguish them, despite the ritual multiplication of the former, make up only one. The former, that of the Supper, pledges and demands the latter; the latter, that of the Cross, fills with historical reality the tenuous ceremonial framework of the former. The Cross is all-important, because our salvation was dependent on it; but the Supper made the Cross inevitable, and therefore in its own way supports it in its turn."

Once the connection between the Supper and the Cross, as single events in time and place, is understood, it is easier to see the continuing relationship of daily Masses all over the world with the unique sacrifice on Calvary; yet it is difficult to write of this relationship without using strictly theological language. It is even dangerous, for an unintentionally ambiguous expression may lead to a misunderstanding of the central truth of Christianity; and it is from such misunderstanding that the heresies and schisms which have destroyed the unity have arisen.

In the later Middle Ages, the popular misconception of this relationship was one of the contributory factors to the Reformation. " It was commonly said " that each Mass was a sacrifice independent of or additional to the sacrifice of the Cross and, further, by identifying the words ' sacrifice ' and ' offering ' with ' bloodshedding,' people came to suppose that Christ was killed afresh at every Eucharist.[1] Against these notions, which they correctly described as " blasphemous fables and dangerous deceits," the English Reformers protested and, in 1553, proclaimed unequivocally: " The offering of Christ once made is the perfect redemption, propitiation and satisfaction for all the sins of the whole world, both original and actual, and there is none other satisfaction for sin but that alone."

Nine years later, the Council of Trent formulated its definition, which made perfectly clear the unchanged and unchanging teaching of the Church and implicitly condemned the misunderstandings which the protestant Reformers had explicitly criticised. To avoid error, it is as well to quote a *résumé* of the definition.

" Once only Jesus our God and Lord would offer Himself to God His Father on the altar of the Cross in an oblation involving death so as to effect in that way our eternal redemption. Nevertheless, His priesthood was not to be extinguished by His death, and thus, at the Last Supper, on the night He was betrayed, He desired to leave His Church a visible sacrifice, in accordance with the requirements of our nature, whereby might be represented that bloody sacrifice which He was about to accomplish once for all upon the Cross . . . As priest for ever, therefore, according to the order of Melchisedech, He offered to God His Father His own Body and Blood under the species of bread and wine . . . He had just celebrated the ancient Pasch, the sacrifice offered by the children of

---

[1] And not only uneducated people. Even Cranmer, a trained theologian, wrote: " If they make every day the same oblation and sacrifice for sin that Christ Himself made, and the oblation that He made was His Death, then followeth it of necessity that every day they slay Christ and shed His Blood."

Israel in memory of the exodus; the passage out of Egypt. He instituted a new Pasch. He was Himself this Pasch which the Church should offer by the ministry of her priests in a rite of mystic immolation under visible signs in memory of His passage from this world to His Father on the day when, by the shedding of His Blood, He redeemed us, delivered us from the power of darkness and translated us into His Kingdom.

" In the divine sacrifice which takes place at Mass there is contained and offered in an unbloody manner the same Christ Who in a bloody manner offered Himself on the altar of the Cross . . . The Victim is in fact both on the Cross and on the altar, one and the same. He Who offers to-day by the ministry of His priests is the same Who offered Himself once upon the Cross; only the manner of offering is different."

Or, as St. Thomas Aquinas had put it centuries before, " we should not say that Christ is crucified or done to death daily. None of these terms, which describe the Jews' treatment of Christ, signifies what takes place daily on the altar. But terms such as ' offer,' ' sacrifice ' or others like them which express Christ's relation to His Father (on the Cross, that is in His priestly office) are applicable to what is effected every morning," giving as the reason that " this Host is perpetual and was offered once by Christ in such a way that it can be offered every day by His members."

(iii) " In remembrance of Me "

The meaning of the Eucharist, in this aspect, is reinforced by the words ' in remembrance of Me,' but by an irony of language the very word which should emphasise the truth actually, because of the associations it has gathered, tends to obscure it. What exactly does 'remembrance' mean? As a translation of the Greek word *anamnesis* it is so unsatisfactory that many prefer to use the Greek to avoid misunderstanding. For us 'remembrance' is inevitably associated with 'remembrance of things past' or of people absent. It is mental recollection of something which is not there. Indeed, it might even be said that 'remembrance' postulates 'absence.' But, as Dom Gregory Dix says in *The Shape of the Liturgy*, "in the Scriptures both of the Old and the New Testament, *anamnesis* and the cognate verb have the sense of 're-calling' or 're-presenting' before God an event in the past, so that it becomes *here and now operative by its effects*." A clear example is the sacrifice made by a wife accused of adultery, under the old Law, as it is laid down in the book of Numbers. She makes an offering "re-calling her sin," that is to say, if she has sinned in the past it will now be revealed by the ordeal because that sin has been actively 're-presented' before God in her sacrifice. "It is in this active sense of 're-calling' or 're-presenting' before God the sacrifice of Christ, and thus making it here and now operative by its effects in the communicants that the Eucharist is regarded both by the New Testament and by second century writers as the *anamnesis* of the Passion, or of the Passion and Resurrection combined."

It is impossible to stress this point too strongly, for what the Mass is emphatically *not* is the memory of the sacrifice of Christ as an historical event in the past. It is the presentation to the Father of the total Christ—crucified, resurrected and ascended—*now*. One has only to read the early Fathers, as Dom Gregory says, " to recognise how completely they identify the offering of the Eucharist by the Church with the offering of Himself by our Lord, not by way of a repetition, but as a ' re-presentation ' (anamnesis) of *the same offering* by the Church ' which is His Body.' As St. Cyprian put it tersely but decisively in the third century: " The Passion is the Lord's Sacrifice which we offer."

THE UNDE ET MEMORES

Wherefore, O Lord, we Thy servants, as also Thy holy people, calling to mind (making an *anamnesis* of) the blessed Passion of Christ Thy Son our Lord, as also His Resurrection from the dead and his glorious Ascension into Heaven, offer unto Thine excellent Majesty from what Thou hast Thyself given and granted, a Sacrifice that is pure, that is holy, that is unblemished —the holy Bread of eternal life and the Chalice of everlasting salvation.

Unde et memores, Domine, nos servi tui, sed et plebs tua sancta, ejusdem Christi Filii tui Domini nostri tam beatae Passionis, necnon et ab inferis Resurrectionis, sed et in caelos gloriosiae Ascensionis, offerimus praeclarae Majestati tuae de tuis donis ac datis, Hostiam puram, Hostiam sanctam, Hostiam immaculatam, Panem sanctum vitae aeternae, et Calicem salutis perpetuae.

(i) *The Purpose of the Prayer*

WHAT IS implicit in the *Qui Pridie*, the ' prayer of Consecration ', is now made explicit in the *Unde et memores*, the ' prayer of Oblation '—the central sacrificial prayer of the Mass. We define what we do. ' Making the anamnesis . . . we offer . . .'' This prayer, with the exception of the Institution-narrative, is the oldest part of the Canon, found in almost identical words even in local deviations from the

103

Roman rite in the second century. Taken with the *Supra Quae* and the *Supplices*, which follow it—the three are really a single prayer—it states with exactitude the meaning of the Mass.

This 'second half' of the Eucharistic Prayer is found in varying forms in the East as well as the West—in Egypt and Syria no less than in Rome. The Eastern forms vary in detail both from each other and from the Western, but the basic pattern is common to all. They define the meaning of what the Church does at the Eucharist and relate it to what was done at the Last Supper. " This is what the Church does at the Eucharist—*offers and communicates*; and it is this which the ' second half' of the prayer expresses and defines. It looks back to the offertory and expresses in words the meaning of that. It looks forward to the communion and prays for the effects of that.[1] It is the function of the prayer to state the meaning of the whole rite." The Celebrant and his assistants (" we Thy servants ") with the congregation present and, by extension, the whole Church Militant on earth, (" Thy holy people "), offer Christ to the Father. And the Christ of the *anamnesis* is not only the Church of the Cross: He is also the Christ of the Resurrection and Ascension. This must be so for, from the point of view of eternity, the " It is finished " of the Cross, the Resurrection and the Ascension, are as a single moment—the moment of the Son's offering and the Father's acceptance. Now, as the Sacramental Body of Christ is on the altar, the Mystical Body of Christ—the Church—makes *anamnesis* of the Incarnate Body, which is resurrected and glorified in heaven.

---

[1] In the Canon this occurs in the *Supplices*. See p. 132.

The familiar lines of a hymn indicate with admirable simplicity this relationship of the three bodies of Christ:

> His Manhood pleads where now it lives
> On Heaven's eternal throne
> And where in mystic rite He gives
> Its presence to His own.

Yet, in meditations on the prayer, it is well to recall something of the meaning of the Resurrection and the Ascension in themselves, for this is their place in the Liturgy.

(ii) The Resurrection

" No doctrine of the Christian faith," said St. Augustine, " is so vehemently and obstinately opposed as the doctrine of the resurrection of the flesh." Long before his day that was true; and the attack has continued remorselessly into our own. Even in certain circles which like to describe themselves as ' christian ' rather than as materialist or pantheist or rationalist, the Resurrection of Christ is explained as ' symbolic ' rather than actual and our own eventual resurrection, which is dependent on it, equated with an impersonal and non-bodily survival.

Nor is the vehemence of the assault surprising, for the Resurrection is the foundation-stone of the Faith. If that goes, the rest collapses. " If Christ be not risen again," as St. Paul insisted, " then is our preaching vain and your faith also is vain." The ' good news ' which from the beginning the apostles asserted was simply the fact of the Resurrection. That was and is ' the gospel ' and the ' apostles ' were, by definition, men who had personal evidence of it and could thus witness to it from their own experience.

Within a few days of Christ's death and burial, they had met Him alive in His body as they could recognise it, bearing still the marks of His suffering. They had spoken to Him, walked with Him, eaten with Him. They had questioned and He had answered. One had doubted and He had given him His body to touch. They had seen the empty tomb where the grave-clothes lay undisturbed; they had breakfasted with Him at a camp-fire on the shores of the lake where He had first called them to follow Him. And so, in the city where He had been killed and to the very people who had condemned Him, they cried: " The God of our fathers raised up Jesus Whom ye slew and hanged on a tree, and we are witnesses to these things." Within two months of the Crucifixion, they had made in Jerusalem more than five thousand converts. In Jerusalem, at least, there was no contradiction. The tomb was there for a visit and a verification. The authorities had but to demonstrate that the crucified ' King of the Jews ' still lay in death where he had been buried. But there was no such answer as " with great power gave the Apostles witness of the Resurrection of the Lord Jesus."

It is well to try to regain something of this original perspective, for the familiarity of the story as a whole dictates to our thought the chronological order—Nativity, the Sermon on the Mount, the parables and the miracles, the trial and the death, the Resurrection and the Ascension—forgetting that this is not the order of historical understanding. There, it is the apostles, inspired and strengthened by the Holy Spirit, excitedly proclaiming the miracle of the Resurrection, which not only overturns all the accepted values of human life, but involves for them and their contemporaries a reinterpretation of the life and death of Jesus. The Resurrection, so to say, makes the birth the Nativity.

And so it is still for the individual facing the fact of it. Even to those brought up in the faith, it is the *realisation* of the Resurrection which illumines conduct. For either the fact is true or it is not. If it is not, then indeed " let us eat, drink and be merry, for tomorrow we die," for death is the master and his slaves are surely entitled to what little amusement they may extract in the course of their long dying. Morality is a mere matter of convenience, a social convention or an accident of geography. One may discuss, for example, the ' ethics ' of divorce or suicide—unlike the Christians for whom, even on a practical level, such talk is barren, since suicide is ultimately no escape and divorce no separation. This is why the Church, in making pronouncements on public topics, is so often incomprehensible to the world. The oft-hurled epithets ' reactionary,' ' narrow,' ' out of touch with life ' are only another way of saying that the Church believes in the Resurrection and the world does not.[1] The humanitarian condemning, for instance, war and capital punishment will—by an unparalleled paradox of language—stigmatize as ' unchristian ' the Christian who, unable to give to death the absolute value he gives it, may question the validity of his conclusions. St. Hugh's famous " The Christian contemplates life with patience and death with desire " is not a ' defeatest

---

[1] A recent and revealing example was the outcry about the Church's teaching concerning deaths in childbirth.

death-wish '; it is a triumphant assertion of the meaning of the Resurrection.

The Resurrection is the inauguration of a new order of life. The apostles insisted, truly, that it was the first event of its kind in the history of the world. It had nothing to do with the ideas of ' survival ' which were quite as prevalent then as now. " It must be clearly understood," as C. S. Lewis has expressed it, " that if the Psychical Researchers succeeded in proving ' survival ' and showed that the Resurrection was an instance of it, they would not be supporting the Christian Faith but refuting it." The Resurrection was a *reversal*. The inevitable process of decay—the ruinousness and futility of Nature ' running down,' so to speak—had been reversed; a new nature, with different laws, had been revealed and of this new nature, by virtue of Christ's defeat of death, mankind was to partake *in the body*.

One consequence of the Resurrection of the Body which non-Christians usually overlook is that it conditions Christian sexual morality. Christian asceticism has nothing in common with the self-denying creeds which, regarding the flesh as something evil, attempt by mortifications to ' escape from the body.' On the contrary, the discipline imposed by the Christian is rather that of the athlete who cares for his body precisely because it is the instrument of his triumph. The nature of the Resurrection-body we cannot know, except that it will be in some way related to the earthly body; and the implications of this relationship have been well expressed by Coventry Patmore in a verse of his *The Victories of Love*, where he speaks of the body with its five senses under the image of a ' five-stringed lyre.'

Beware: for fiends in triumph laugh
O'er him who learns the truth by half!
Beware; for God will not endure
For men to make their hope more pure
Than His good promise, or require
Another than the five-stringed lyre
Which He has vowed again to the hands
Devout of him who understands
To tune it justly here.

But this, as well as many other consequences in conduct, belongs rather to the realm of moral theology than to a consideration of the Mass (except, of course, insofar as all ' christian morality ' is not a code but personal behaviour springing from participation in the Eucharist). What, at this moment in the Canon dominates devotion, is the Resurrection itself, the new creation inaugurated when " this Man, after He had offered one sacrifice for sins for ever, sat down at the right hand of God."

(iii) The Ascension

The moment—in time—of the taking up of the Body into the Godhead is known as the Ascension. " Christ," as one of the Articles of the Church of England puts it, reflecting all traditional teaching, " took again His body, with flesh, bones and all things appertaining to the perfection of man's nature, wherewith He ascended into Heaven and there sitteth." This definition was necessitated by Luther's mistake that, as a result of the Ascension, Christ's body became omnipresent. Since this particular misunderstanding is still rife in the kind of untheological piety which speaks of the presence of 'Jesus' (in contradistinction to God) in a room or on a hillside or in the street, it is necessary to stress that Jesus's body is in heaven and that it is unique. Not only is 'omnipresence' contrary to the plain teaching of the apostles, the New Testament and the three creeds of the undivided Church,[1] but, by implication, it contradicts the very meaning of the Incarnation. Even on the lower level of logic, it is easily disposed of since " a humanity that is of itself and unconditionally omnipresent would hardly be human any longer." The mode of Jesus's presence on earth is in his Sacramental Body—" on the Cross the Godhead alone was hidden: here even the Humanity is concealed "—and in his Mystical Body, the Church, the human vessel of the Holy Spirit. The mere statement of this is, perhaps, enough to explain why the particular movement which impugned both the Bodies was forced to invent 'omnipresence' to account for any continuing relationship at all between the risen Lord and the world He left when He returned to the Father, " taking the Manhood into God."

In the primitive Christian teaching which is enshrined in the Canon of the Mass, the thought immediately recalled by the Ascension is the analogy insisted on in the *Epistle to the Hebrews*: " The first covenant had also ordinances of divine service and a worldly sanctuary. For there was a tabernacle made; the first, wherein was the candlestick and the table and the shewbread; which is called the sanctuary. And after the second veil the tabernacle, which is called the Holy of

---

[1] The Apostles' Creed, the Nicene Creed and the Athanasian Creed all insist in the same language that Jesus ' sitteth at the right hand of God ' whence He will return to earth for the last Judgment.

Holies . . . Now when these things were thus ordained, the priests went always into the first tabernacle, accomplishing the service of God; but into the second went the High Priest alone once every year, not without blood, which he offered for himself and for the sins of the people . . . But Christ being come an High Priest of good things to come, by a greater and more perfect tabernacle, not made with hands, that is to say, not of this building; neither by the blood of goats and calves, but by His own blood, he entered once into the Holy Place, having obtained eternal redemption for us . . . For Christ is not entered into the holy places made with hands, which are the figures of the true, but into Heaven itself, now to appear in the presence of God for us . . . Having therefore, brethren, boldness to enter into the Holiest by the blood of Jesus, by a new and living way which He hath consecrated for us, through the veil, that is, His Flesh, and having an High Priest over the house of God, let us draw near with a true heart and full assurance of faith."

Yet the Christian to-day, however firm his faith and however simply he comes, in this faith, to the altar, is faced, in the controversy of the world, with the difficulty of reconciling the truth as expressed in *Hebrews* with what are called ' the scientific findings about the nature of the physical universe.' Where, in fact, is ' heaven ' ? When the disciples watched Jesus go ' up ' till a cloud received him out of their sight, they were thinking in terms of an ' earth ' that was flat and a ' heaven ' which was a kind of ' upper story ' out of sight above the sky. Such a mental picture is impossible for scientifically-educated men to-day.[1]

[1] Though not, one is tempted to think, for 90 per cent of mankind.

The obvious answer to this, which Dr. Swete gives in *The Ascended Christ*, is that " a conception which limits His ascent to any region, however remote from earth, or locates His ascended life in any part of the material universe, falls vastly short of the primitive belief; no third heaven, no seventh heaven of Jewish speculation, no central sun of later conjecture, meets the requirements of an exaltation to the Throne of God." And the language of the New Testament writers makes it clear that, to them at least, it was so. To St. Paul, Jesus ascended ' far above all the heavens ': St. John insists that, at the Last Supper, he declared that He was about to leave the ' world of created things.'[1]

It is in this language that the real answer lies—for that answer is bound to insist that the Ascension raises issues as acute as those of the Resurrection and in neither case can the Christian meet the world with a compromising ' symbolism.' As the Resurrection inaugurates a new nature, so the Ascension is a further manifestation of its existence. Put in the simplest terms, the resurrected body must have gone *somewhere*. To quote C. S. Lewis again: " We must indeed believe the risen body to be extremely different from the mortal body, but the existence, in that new state of anything that could in any sense be described as ' body ' at all involves some sort of spatial relationship and, in the long run, a whole new universe."

We can agree with the scientists that there is no question of a human body, as we know it, existing in interstellar space, as we know it, while at the same time insisting that this in no way affects the Ascension in its literal and simple sense. For the ' as we know it ' is a reminder that all that science can

[1] This is the force of the Greek word translated ' world ' in John 16, 29.

ever offer is an ' interim report ': final truth is that of revelation. " A man who really believes that ' Heaven ' is in the
sky may well, in his heart, have a far truer and more spiritual
conception of it than many a modern logician who could
expose that fallacy with a few strokes of his pen. For he who
does the will of the Father shall know the doctrine . . . When
God made space and worlds that move in space, and clothed
our world with air, and gave us such eyes and such imaginations as those we have, He knew what the sky would mean
to us. And since nothing in His work is accidental, if He
knew, He intended. We cannot be certain that this was not
indeed one of the chief purposes for which Nature was created;
still less that it was not one of the chief reasons why the
Ascension was allowed to affect human senses as a movement
upwards."

To look on the Ascension as a child might understand it
when being told the story for the first time or as the great
artists represented it, is still permissible to the Christian mind.
And, in the end, it is the safest; for any other idea of it rests,
in the last analysis, on that most untenable of all beliefs, the
belief that man is omniscient and his intellect infallible.

(iv) The Transformation of the Gift

Having made the *anamnesis* of the Christ of the completed
sacrifice—crucified, risen, ascended—we return to him in his
mode of sacrifice on the altar. The words used to describe
the Host are chosen with precision—pure, holy and unblemished—for the thought is still, on the one hand, on the
analogy of previous sacrifices and, on the other, on the person

of Christ. So we think of the Sacrifice as pure, in contra-distinction to those of the pagans, which were unclean and corrupt; as holy, in contradistinction to those of the Jews which, though indeed ordained by God, were mere fore-shadowings, imperfect in their effects—" for the Law made nothing perfect," to quote *Hebrews* again, " but the bringing-in of a better hope did by the which we draw nigh unto God ";—as unblemished because there is only one spotless sacrifice and 'none other good enough to pay the price of sin.' But we also see it as " pure, because it was conceived by the Holy Spirit; holy, because it is united personally to the Word; immaculate, because, freed from mortality, it has passed to a state of glorification."

The fivefold sign of the Cross, indicative of the five wounds of Christ, which are made here, recall those made in the *Quam Oblationem*. As I put it earlier, as they are the last signature on the bread and wine, they are the first on the Body and Blood. As the five wounds were, so to speak, the sign-manual of the sacrifice, authenticating that the resurrected body, which had experienced death, was indeed the same that had hung, pierced, on the Cross, so this symbolising of those five wounds bridges another mystical transition. The gesture inevitably recalls the words of the earlier prayer to which these are an answer. We prayed that God would make our offering of bread and wine ' blessed, approved, ratified, reasonable and acceptable.' Now he has given it back to us ' pure, holy and unblemished.'

We are careful not to forget that in both cases we can offer only what he has given us. The natural bounties of the earth and the strength and joy of human life, summed up in

the first offering, are no less his gift to us than t
Bread of eternal life and Chalice of everlasting salv.
the second. *Tuis donis ac datis*—'from what thou hast thyself
given and granted.' All we can ever do is to *render*, not to
give, and now, above all, is the moment to remember it.

Render means 'give back.' The word is used only twice
in the gospels and then in a single context. The parable of the
wicked husbandmen who refused to render to the landlord
the rights on his own estate was told by Jesus just before he
was asked that question·about the tribute money to which
he replied "Render into Caesar the things that are Caesar's
and unto God the things that are God's." In the ordinary
way of civilization, Caesar was only demanding what was
his due. The coin, stamped with his image, announced the
overlordship of the *Pax Romana* with all its amenities of a
peaceful life of which the questioners took full advantage in
pursuit of their day-to-day interests. It was only right that,
by giving back the coin to Caesar in the way of tax, they
should pay for those privileges. Yet the claims of Caesar are
reduced to practical insignificance by comparison with the
immensity of ' Give back to God the things that are God's ';
for that is life itself and the whole of living—body, soul and
spirit. It is this we do in fact ' give back ' in the offertory of
the Eucharist, (which, on our part, is, among other things,
our explicit repudiation of the ethics of a Caesar-conscious
world.) This particular incident has a double relevance here
because, in the interim between the Last Supper and the
Crucifixion, Jesus pointed the meaning when He replied to
Caesar's deputy. Pilate's: "Knowest Thou not that I have
power to crucify Thee and have power to release Thee?"

was answered by "Thou couldst have no power at all against Me, except it were given thee from above."

Thus *tuis dodis ac datis* becomes a matter-of-fact statement of reality. Though the phrase defines the basis and meaning of humility, it cannot even properly be called a protestation of it, for this would imply an egocentricity entirely absent from this prayer, in which, as Zundel puts it, " the Church has found language miraculously bare into which self cannot intrude at any point. When the eternal Word is uttered by the lips of sinful man, it would have been so easy to burst out into protestations of unworthiness and evoke the awe of the prophets confronted with the Divine glory. But since it is God Who has willed the condescension, it is far simpler to take refuge in the wisdom of His love. We have remembered Thy command and we have *obeyed* it in memory of Thee."

THE SUPRA QUAE

Upon which vouchsafe to look with a kind and serene countenance and to accept them, even as Thou once didst graciously hold accepted the gifts of Thy just servant Abel, the sacrifice of our Patriarch Abraham and that which Thy high priest Melchisedech offered to Thee, a holy sacrifice, an unblemished victim.

Supra quae propitio ac sereno vultu respicere digneris, et accepta habere, sicuti accepta habere dignatus es munera pueri tui justi Abel, et sacrificium Patriarchae nostri Abrahae: et quod tibi obtulit summus sacerdos tuus Melchisedech, sanctum sacrificium, immaculatam hostiam.

IT HAS been said of the *Supra Quae* that " these few words bring before us the entire course of religion, its continuity from first to last, the mysterious unity of history, the spiritual meaning of the universe, the perpetuity of hope and the eternity of love." This short prayer is explicitly concerned with the meaning of sacrifice; it is the full statement of the theme announced in the *Te Igitur*. I mentioned earlier how the prayer for acceptance, which opens the Canon, " appears even in the *Supra Quae* after the Consecration " (and is necessitated because our offering is that of the Perfect Christ and of our imperfect selves *in one*).[1] And to understand this prayer the simple outline of sacrifice which I give there must now be filled in.

(i) *Sacrifice as Adoration*

Man, when he offers sacrifice, intends to make something sacred by giving it unconditionally to God and then, by means of it, when it is ' divinised ' entering into a special relationship with God. First, he renounces some treasured personal possession which, though dear to him, belongs, as he himself does, to the world of imperfection. That is *immolation*. Having given up all his rights in the immolated object, he offers it completely to God. That is *oblation*. He then prays for *acceptance by God*, since without it there will be no making sacred and thus no sacrifice. Finally, he must in some way reclaim the offered object, now ' charged with the divine acceptance ' that it may be his bond of at-one-ment with God. That is *communion*.

These ideas are common to all religions and so can be truly described as epitomising ' the entire course of religion.' More-over, what underlies them, may properly be called a vision of " the spiritual meaning of the universe, the perpetuity of hope and the eternity of love." For man's instinct to sacrifice, from the very dawn of time, is based on a perception (not, of course, articulated intellectually) of God's order of the universe, and is an attempt, hoping beyond apparent failure, to co-operate successfully in it. Since God has placed in all His creatures a continuous movement towards himself, man must,

---

[1] See p. 39.

if he is to be true to his own nature, perpetually assert this in face of the disorder and chaos around him. Surrounded by human meaninglessness, he is yet bound to proclaim the divine meaning.

"Sacrifice," says St. Thomas Aquinas, "puts before our eyes the directing of the mind to God . . . For the proper directing of the mind to God, man must recognize that the goods which he possesses come from God as first principle, and he must relate them to God as the last end. And that is why man in offering sacrifices avowed that God was the first principle of the world's creation and the last end to whom all must be related . . . For the intelligence to be properly related to God, it must recognize no other original author but God and place its last end in Him alone."

Or, as Pierre Termier has more picturesquely expressed it: "There have always been worshippers, suppliants, lovers . . . That has been enough for God. As the earth turns around the sun times without number, many crimes are committed on its surface, many bestial cries, shouts of grief and despair, even blasphemies, rise from this strangely-fated planet to the horror-stricken skies; but the holy murmur from retreats where simple, good men are praying easily drown the shouting and the blasphemy; and the smoke of sacrifice, a thin blue column rising into the calm air of dawn or dusk, bears a perfume so keen that it destroys the stench of the crimes."

Thus, by sacrifice man asserts the divine order of the universe. He becomes, by a deliberate act of will, God's collaborator. "Sacrifice is an action," says Dom Eugène Masure, "accomplished through the creature's efforts, making its own drive to its end under the almighty act of God." And this assertion of the Divine order is, necessarily, an act of adoration. It is " the entire movement of our created nature . . . the creature giving itself and reaching God in a great impact in which our deepest needs are satisfied."

The *expression* of this adoration has, in the story of mankind, certainly appeared often as a most repulsive and bloodthirsty rite. The ghastly holocausts of paganism from the slaughters of Rome to the shambles of Mexico; the continuing blood-shedding of primitive tribes and the customs of the ancients enshrined in the classics are sufficient to sicken the mind unless the motive behind them is understood, and we can see beneath the rubbish heap of myths, rites, weird confusions and hideous practices, the line of the movement toward God.

Yet why does ' immolation ' imply death? Can that be God's will? Can He take pleasure in the extinction of the life He made? Could He in any sense welcome the death of his Son? To put the questions is to answer them. It was Christ's obedience, not his death, which was pleasing to God. It was the world of fallen humanity, not God, which made the Cross the price of His obedience. Long ago, even before Calvary, the *Wisdom of Solomon* had faced that issue: " God did not make death and He feels no joy at the loss of living. He has created all things for life . . . God created men for immortality and He has made them in the image of His own Nature. It is by envy of the Devil that sin has come into the world." Sin, entering Eden, brought with it grief and death. " Offering our life to God in Eden would have been a prayer, a thing supremely sweet: to-day this encounter is called the world over by the name of death." But it is still the offering of life, not the encounter of death, which lies behind it all. " Give Me your life as it is," says Christ in the Mass, " and I will make it My Life as it is."

(ii) Abel, Abraham, Melchisedech

Of the many ways of regarding the Old Testament, the wisest is to see it as the book which Christ knew in his human life. Its theology, its literature, its history were his formative reading. The psalms were *his* hymnbook—a fact sometimes forgotten, it would seem, by those who try to edit the ethics of them—as the prophets, humanly speaking, were his inspiration. And the names of the great exemplars of sacrifice, Abel, Abraham and Melchisedech were the currency of his nation's history.

They were, of course, much more than this, for He knew them in his manhood as foretypes of Himself. The tremendous claim: " Before Abraham was I am "; the indictment of the persecuting Jews responsible for shedding innocent blood since the beginning of time—" from the blood of the righteous Abel "; the reference to the ' Melchisedech ' Psalm in an argument in which " no man was able to answer Him a word, neither durst any man from that day forth ask Him any more questions,"[1]—these are known moments in his ministry. But before the manhood was the childhood, in which he would learn—like other children of his day and ours—the Bible stories about the three.

" Abel was a keeper of sheep but Cain was a tiller of the

---

[1] In this argument (Matthew 22, 41 *et seq.*) he is referring indeed only to the first of the seven short verses of Psalm 110; but the Melchisedech reference is inescapably relevant to the occasion and must have been in everyone's mind.

ground. And in process of time it came to pass that Cain brought the fruit of the ground an offering to the Lord. And Abel, he also brought of the firstlings of his flock and of the fat thereof. And the Lord had respect unto Abel and to his offering: but to Cain and his offering he had not respect. And Cain was very wroth . . . and Cain rose up against Abel his brother and slew him."

" Abraham took the wood of the burnt offering and laid it upon Isaac his son; and he took the fire in his hand and a knife; and they went both of them together. And Isaac spake unto Abraham his father and said: My Father, and he said, Here am I, my son. And he said. Behold the fire and the wood: but where is a lamb for the burnt offering? And Abraham said, My son, God will provide himself a lamb for a burnt offering: so they went both of them together. And they came to the place which God had told him of; and Abraham built an altar there, and laid the wood in order, and bound Isaac his son, and laid him on the altar upon the wood. And Abraham stretched forth his hand and took the knife to slay his son. And the angel of the Lord called unto him out of heaven and said: Abraham, Abraham: and he said, Here am I. And he said, Lay not thine hand upon the lad, neither do thou anything unto him: for now I know that thou fearest God, seeing thou hast not withheld thy son, thine only son from me. And Abraham lifted up his eyes and looked, and behold behind him a ram caught in a thicket by his horns: and Abraham went and took the ram, and offered him up for a burnt offering in the stead of his son."

" After Abraham's slaughter of Chedorlaomer and of the kings that were confederate with him, the King of Sodom went out to meet him at the valley of Shaveh, which is the King's Dale. And Melchisedech, King of Salem, brought forth bread and wine: and he was the priest of the most high God. And he blessed him . . . and he gave him tithes of all."

Those are the stories of the three sacrificers as told in the book of Genesis and it is perhaps worth remembering that, though scholars have been able to analyse the book into its four basic narratives, there is one fragment of it which remains unaccountable and unaccounted for—the chapter about Melchisedech. Even on a literary and critical plane, he is a mystery. And, with the single exception of the reference in Psalm 110: "The Lord hath sworn and will not repent, Thou art a priest for ever after the order of Melchisedech," he is not again mentioned until *Hebrews* elaborates his relevance to Jesus " made an high priest for ever after the order of Melchisedech. For this Melchisedech, king of Salem, priest of the most high God, who met Abraham returning from the slaughter of the kings, and blessed him; to whom also Abraham gave a tenth part of all: first, being by interpretation King of Righteousness, and after that also King of Salem, which is King of Peace; without father, without mother, without descent, having neither beginning of days nor end of life; but made like unto the Son of God; abideth a priest continually."

Even the reference in the *Supra Quae*, like the reference in *Genesis*, postulates a literary and critical problem. The Canon refers to *summus sacerdos tuus Melchisedech*, ' Thy high priest Melchisedech '; but in the Bible he is the ' priest of the most high God.' One of this century's great commentators on the Liturgy, Anton Baumstark, used this difference in an argument

which suggested that the Latin Canon of the Mass was a
translation from an original Greek Canon and that "the
translator, foundering on the difficulties of the Greek form, of
words, made of a 'Priest of God Most High' a 'Most High
Priest of God.'" Other scholars have, for various reasons,
decided against this—for one reason, the Latin Bible already
had the form used in the Canon; for another, as early as
A.D. 380 Melchisedech was termed 'high priest' in the Greek-
speaking East—but the change, for whatever reason it was
originally made, indicates a devotional perception. For
Melchisedech, whoever he may have been, has become simply
a foretype of the Great High Priest. With his 'bread and
wine,' he is that essentially.

The symbolism of the three interlocks in various ways.
Melchisedech stands as representative of the Gentiles as
Abraham of the Jews and Abel of all mankind. Abraham's
son, Isaac, is an even more definite foretype of Christ than is
Melchisedech; and Isaac's blood flowed in Jesus's veins. The
allusiveness of Abraham's "My son, God will provide a
lamb" is as inescapable as the elements of Melchisedech's
oblation—bread and wine. The first-fruits of the first sacrificer,
Abel, recall him who is 'first-born among his brethren' and
'first-fruits of them that slept.'

Yet, though this passage provides a meditative commentary
on sacrifice, the reasons for the naming of the three goes far
deeper. The point at issue is the acceptability of their sacrifices.
The discrimination between Cain's offering and Abel's was
that Cain's cost nothing. Abraham's trial of faith was something even more than that demanded by the ghastly death of
his son, for that death seemed to make everything he had

lived by a mockery. Not only, as we might stress it in this later age, about the nature of God; but about the very fact of God. God had promised him that his seed should outnumber the sands of the sea and the boy Isaac was his only son, born when his wife was old. The demand for his life, in that fashion and at that time, might well have provoked Abraham to imagine that he had been communing with some devil of his own distorted imagination. Yet "by faith Abraham, when he was tried, offered up Isaac; and he that had received the promises offered up his only begotten son, of whom it was said that 'in Isaac shall thy seed be called,' accounting that God was able to raise him up, even from the dead." Melchisedech's bread and wine, though so simple and so different from the ideas of sacrifice of that age, were wholly acceptable in that, by a kind of mystical perception, that 'king of righteousness' and 'king of peace' anticipated the offering of Another.

Thus we pray, in so far as we ourselves are included in the Oblation, that our intentions may be perfect as those of Abel, Abraham and Melchisedech, and that He who accepted their sacrifices will, a *fortiori*, accept what, because It is his Son, is 'a holy sacrifice, an unblemished victim.'[1]

---

[1] It seems more reasonable to apply the words ' sanctum sacrificium, immaculatam hostiam ' to the Host than to Melchisedech's offering, as the Latin grammatically allows and as is done in some translations. The four words were added to the original prayer by Pope Leo the Great (died 461).

THE SUPPLICES

      ·

We most humbly beseech Thee, almighty God, to command that
these things be carried up by the hands of Thy holy angel to
Thine altar on high, in the sight of Thy divine majesty, that so
many of us as are partakers of the precious Body and Blood of
Thy Son at this altar may be filled with all heavenly benediction
and grace. Through the same Christ our Lord. Amen.

Supplices te rogamus, omnipotens Deus: jube haec preferri per
manus sancti Angeli tui in sublime altare tuum, in conspectu
divinae majestatis tuae: ut quotquot ex hac altaris participatione
sacrosanctum Filii tui Corpus et Sanguinem sumpserimus, omni
benedictione coelesti et gratia repleamur. Per eumdem Christum
Dominum nostrum. Amen.

(i) " Our exalted brothers, the Angels "

ALL LIFE and goodness and beauty in this world are " imaged
shatterings of that majestic perfection " which is God.
Among created beings, the closest resemblance to the Creator
is found in " our exalted brothers, the Angels." Each a pure
spirit, ageless, immortal, differing from his fellows, not as
one man differs from another, but as one species differs from
another—as a rose differs from a lion—the hierarchy of angels
fills the universe with a splendour beyond imagination.
Beyond imagination, literally. Our failure in practice to give
due weight to the doctrine of the existence of angels is a

weakness of imagination, not a difficulty of reason. We know enough of the countless gradations of life-forms descending from man to the protoplasm for our intellect to demand similar ranks of created beings to bridge the gulf between man and deity. "Why," as Bishop Talbot asked, "should we admit that nature below us teems with life and yet predicate an absolute blank between ourselves and God? Why should the exuberant fertility of the great Creator be arrested at that point when Man appears upon the scene and first unites in himself the material and the physical?" Yet our imagination so far lags behind our logic that the modern world stands rather with Pascal, looking at the lonely stars and terrified by the infinite spaces, than with the early Christians who saw the stars as symbols of the angels and knew that, once at least, over the Bethlehem fields, the Angelic Gloria had broken the silence.

The failure to imagine has been reflected in the failure to represent. Since it is an essential quality of an angel to be bodiless, the artist is, in a sense, foredoomed to failure. Indeed, the Church for the first seven centuries forbade any attempt at representation. Only at the Second Council of Nicaea in 787—that is to say, nearly two centuries after this prayer was composed—was it allowed, in view of the many cases in Scripture where an angel, in his capacity as messenger, had assumed a recognizable form, that "angels have the human form and may be so represented."[1] And in the earliest figures

[1] It is, however, important to realise that "angels can assume and have assumed the appearance of bodies; but they have not, as the souls of men do, become the life principle of those assumed 'bodies.' They have not, in other words, denied or cast off the purely spiritual character of their natures. These apparent bodies of angels could not act vitally; even under the guise of a physical form, the angel could not eat, digest, see or hear, generate children. These 'bodies' were tools of the angels, not a living part of them."—Walter Farrell, O.P.

of angels in art, there is rather a stylisation of attributes than an attempt at representation. Yet how can wings really suggest a speed of movement from one material plane to another accomplished with no more effort and in no more time than it takes to move the mind from one subject to another? How can an impassivity of countenance convey the rapt adoration which springs from a " love that matches the most perfect mirroring of divine knowledge?" And as, gradually, the angels in art became divorced from an understanding of theology and from a fervency of faith, so in the popular mind they became beings obviously mythological and faintly grotesque, like full-size and forbidding fairies.

The pen, in this case, is mightier than the brush and something of the true angelic splendour still breaks through St. John's Apocalyptic vision of many angels about the throne, " ten thousand times ten thousand and thousands of thousands, saying with a loud voice: 'Worthy is the Lamb that was slain to receive power and riches and wisdom and strength and glory and honour and blessing,' " while the mind's eye can see more vividly than the artist can paint that angel who " came and stood at the altar, having a golden censer " to whom was given " much incense that he should offer it with the prayers of all saints upon the golden altar which was before the throne."

Though this passage obviously lies behind the thought at the beginning of the *Supplices*, it is only part of the background. The other and the greater concerns an aspect of angels as messengers to the world of men. At every point they appear thus in the Bible story, from the Angel with the Flaming Sword who, on the morrow of the Fall, stood guard over Eden to the Angel of the Agony who, on the eve of the Redemption, consoled Christ in another garden. In Jesus's life on earth, they were never far distant. To his mother, they announced his entry into life; to his friends, his resurrection from the dead. They gloried at his birth in a too-crowded town; they ministered to Him after his trial in a desolate wilderness. Twelve legions were at his call had the burden of his suffering broken the steadfastness of His obedience.

And long before his day Isaiah, who had seen the Seraphim and heard them cry: ' Holy, holy, holy is the Lord of Hosts: the whole earth is full of his glory! ' understood that one of the names of Messiah himself would be the Angel of Great Counsel. In the more familiar English version of the Bible, this is rendered as ' counseller ': " For unto us a child is born, unto us a son is given; and the government shall be on his shoulder; and his name shall be called Wonderful, Counseller, the Mighty God, the Everlasting Father, the Prince of Peace." This verse forms part of the Introit for the Dawn Mass of Christmas and the old Roman version of the Old Testament translate it, perceptively as *magni consilii angelus*, the Angel of Great Counsel—and it is this Angel, Christ Himself, who in our prayer is the bearer of the gifts to the heights of heaven.

In the earliest version of the *Supplices*, in the fourth century, the hands are those of the angels in general (*per manus angelorum tuorum*), but already, before the end of the sixth century, the thought of the Church had insisted on an individual action and, though in the earliest devotion it tended to be ascribed to the Angel of Incense whose gift was offered with ' the prayers of all saints,' the interpretation that it was

Christ, the Angel of Great Counsel, was already established by the twelfth century.

If this line of devotion be followed, there is a moving parallelism of thought between this moment of the Canon and the *Sanctus* and *Benedictus* which immediately precede it. As the end of the *Preface*, with its majestic reminder of the hierarchy of the angels—" Through Christ our Lord, through whom the angels praise Thy majesty, the Dominions worship it, the Powers stand in awe; the heavens and the heavenly hosts and the blessed Seraphim together join in celebrating their joy "—leads to Isaiah's awestruck vision and the sound of " Holy, holy, holy " but finds its climax in the shout of children welcoming a Man on a donkey: " Blessed is He that cometh in the name of the Lord," so here the glimpse of the splendour of heaven is connected, for those who follow the Church's worship, with the poverty of Bethlehem.

And perhaps, after all, it does not matter overmuch that few of the ' wise ' could name the nine choirs of the host of heaven—the three contemplative orders: the Seraphim, ' exceeding, in love '; the Cherubim, with their perfect knowledge; the Thrones, with their perception of order; the three regulative orders of Dominations and Virtues and Powers; and the three administrative orders: Principalities, Archangels and Angels—as long as the many simple know and pause when they hear the bell for *Angelus*.

(ii) " This Altar "

The priest says this supplicatory prayer bowing low over

the altar and when he reaches the words " partakers . . . of this altar " he kisses it. But words, gesture and action refer not merely to the visible altar before him; it is now conceived as being one with the ' altar on high.' The Latin words *ex hac altaris participatione* mean ' by this sharing in the altar '; they do not and cannot mean ' by the sharing in this altar ' with reference to the altar close at hand. They indicate specifically that we have a share in the heavenly altar on which our gift is now presumed to lie.

Here, as perhaps nowhere else in the Canon, thought and language fail to convey the full meaning. " The human mind " said Innocent III of this prayer, " can hardly penetrate its sense " nor have the Fathers attempted to explain it. By some it has been conjectured that the ' altar on high ' is the glorified humanity of Jesus " inasmuch as the glory which radiates from His transfigured Humanity is like a hymn of praise and prayer which ever goes up from the altar to heaven reminding the Father of all the merits of the Cross of which this glory is the eternal ratification." Jesus is thus both the gift and the altar and the angel. But the symbolism is not really capable of rationalisation in this way; and, since the deepest minds are baffled, it is perhaps best to regard it as the simple assertion of the identity at this moment of the Host and the Body which inevitably unites earth and heaven, angels and men, and, leaving language, to lean on the sublime simplicity of ritual as the priest's kiss, indicating the identity of the altars, is followed immediately by the three fold cross over the Host, the Chalice and then on himself (as representing the people), betokening the transition to the ' partaking ' of them.

(iii) *Communion*

So the thought of the prayer moves from Consecration to Communion, from sacrifice to sacrament. We come to the final and completing phase of all sacrifice—the return of the gift, accepted and ' divinised '—and look forward to the communion we shall make, when, partaking of that gift, we shall be filled " with all heavenly benediction and grace."

As, in considering the *Quam Oblationem* we saw how an understanding of the Canon nullifies later disagreements about ' Transubstantiation,' so here in the conclusion of the *Supplices* there is indicated the true relationship between sacrifice and sacrament, of which misunderstandings in the past have given rise to divisions hardly less lamentable. As stated here, they are seen as so interdependent that the false conceptions which rest on stressing one at the expense of the other are impossible. The " Holy Sacrifice of the Mass "—the mystical, adoring, Godward action—cannot be separated from " the Lord's Supper "—the practical, saving, man-ward action. " Attending Mass " may, in certain circumstances and for utilitarian reasons, differ from " making one's communion "; but it ought not to. The Reformers' insistence on this matches the constant plea of the Popes who have urged frequent communion and proclaimed that " by receiving Communion the faithful take part in the Sacrifice," for " the Communion belongs to the integration of the Sacrifice."

Always, of course, the celebrant himself communicates on behalf of the people, for no sacrifice is possible without Communion. It would be a contradiction in terms. Yet, at certain times in history, this has been popularly misunderstood and misleading shibboleths have distracted the devout, insinuating a difference where no difference is. A 'non-communicating High Mass,' emphasising the sacrifice, has become erroneously differentiated, almost in kind, from a simple 'Holy Communion' where the worshippers appropriate to themselves the effects of the sacrifice. In the *Supplices*, where the two are brought together, and in the connection of the *Supplices* with the rest of the Canon, the proper relationship is observed and stated and we are thus given one more reminder of the wisdom of Pope Pius X's plea: " Do not pray during Mass; but pray the Mass."

THE MEMENTO ETIAM

Be mindful, O Lord, of Thy servants, men and women, N. and N., who have gone before us with the sign of faith and sleep the sleep of peace. To them, O Lord, and to all who rest in Christ, grant, we beseech Thee a place of refreshing, light and peace, through the same Christ our Lord. Amen.

Memento etiam, Domine, famulorum, famularumque tuarum N. et N., qui nos praecesserunt cum signo fidei et dormiunt in somno pacis. Ipsis, Domine, et omnibus in Christo quiescentibus locum refrigerii, lucis et pacis, ut indulgeas, deprecamur. Per eundem Christum Dominum nostrum. Amen.

THIS IS the prayer for the dead. In the *Memento etiam* we pray for our dead friends as, in the *Memento Domine*, we prayed for those who are alive. As in the former prayer, so now, the celebrant joins his hands in personal intercession, while, at the signal, each member of the congregation remembers his own. The Church Triumphant in heaven and the Church Militant on earth for the moment give place to the Church Expectant—or the Church Suffering—in purgatory. This remembrance of the dead was originally, about the third century, in a different place in the Mass; and in the very earliest times it seems that the dead were commemorated by name only when the Mass was a Requiem said expressly for them. On the other hand, the ritual reading of the names by the deacon which once took place here—the Diptychs of Dead paralleling the Diptychs of the Living—is a later custom to be explained by the Roman insistence on order and symmetry. But what need is there to defend, or to examine the reason for, the stabilisation of the prayer at this particular place, when no more fitting point could be imagined?

Our thought is on Communion, which once those we loved shared with us, and because of *that* Communion we can, as in no other way, still commune with them. " Since their life is plunged deep in the interior of God; since He is their home, their food and, as our prayer so touchingly expresses it, their sleep, if we identify ourselves more closely with Him "—as we are about to do when we receive his body —" we shall enter into their life, and the converse broken off on the visible plane will be resumed in a more living fashion in the silent commerce of souls," says Zundel. " They are in God, the very heart of love. God has not taken them from us: He has hidden them in His heart that they may be closer to ours."

(i) *Purgatory*

The very fact that we pray for our dead assumes that they can benefit from our prayers. Otherwise it is a vain, sentimental self-indulgence whose only effect can be to harm ourselves. But there is no known time when Christians have not so prayed. The doctrine was part of the Church's inheritance from Judaism and still, in the reading for anniversary masses for the dead, the faithful are reminded how, a hundred years before Christ, Judas Maccabeus sent a great sum of money to Jerusalem for sacrifices on behalf of his dead soldiers who had died in sin " doing therein very well and honestly in that he was mindful of the resurrection; for if he had not hoped that they which were slain should have risen again, it had been superfluous and vain to pray for the dead; and also in that he perceived that they who had fallen asleep with godliness had great grace laid up for them. It is therefore a holy and wholesome thought to pray for the dead that they may be loosed from their sins."

In the synagogue worship which Christ attended, prayers for the dead were in use and He Himself, during his ministry, categorically contradicted the Sadducees, who denied survival. " God is not the God of the dead but the God of the living; ye therefore do greatly err." He told the parable of Dives and Lazarus which at least implies a state of consciousness after death in some way dependent on conduct during life. And on the Cross, he promised the penitent thief: " To-day shalt thou be with Me in Paradise."[1]

Inscriptions in the catacombs such as " Intercession has been made for the soul of the dear one departed and God has heard the prayer and the soul has passed into a place of light and refreshment ": the testimony of Tertullian: " We offer oblations for the dead, as birth-day honours ": the rules of St. Cyprian, the explanations of St. Clement of Alexandria, and the Liturgy itself, leave no doubt of the beliefs and

---

[1] Paradise, not Heaven. It is also perhaps worth noting that Christ's words: " And whosoever shall speak a word against the Son of Man, it shall be forgiven him; but he that shall speak against the Holy Ghost, it shall be forgiven him neither in this world nor in the world to come " are interpreted by St. Augustine, St. Gregory the Great, St. Isidore of Seville, St. Bede, St. Bernard and many others as implying a purgatory where sins not forgiven here will be forgiven.

practices of the early Church. There is, indeed, only one writer, Aerius, who opposes such prayers and offerings; and, as he also denied the divinity of Christ and founded a schism of his own, even his testimony is valuable.

One might go even further and say that, were not the doctrine of purgatory so firmly attested, it would have been necessary to postulate it. When we consider, on the one hand, the moral imperfections of so many Christians at death and, on the other, the impossibility of seeing God 'without sanctification,' as *Hebrews* puts it, we are forced to believe in a life beyond the grave which includes a disciplinary purgation of character while the soul awaits the final judgment and its reuniting with the body.

Yet, having insisted on this, it is necessary to insist equally strongly that we know nothing at all of the nature of the purgatorial state. The Church, always careful to make no dogmatic definition on the subject, even went out of her way at the Council of Trent to reprove those who tried to terrify the faithful with fearsome imaginary pictures. Bishops and clergy were bidden " to exclude from their preaching difficult and subtle questions which tend not to edification and from the discussion of which there is no increase either of piety or of devotion." And a ' place of refreshing, light and peace,' as our prayer has it, can still be a state of purgation, since the motive behind the purgation is our own love. Refreshed, we can see the sins that in our tiredness we did not think of as sins; light illumines the dark corners; in peace we dare relinquish the possession of our souls.

In her wisdom, too, the Church leaves open the more personal question as to whether souls in purgatory still know our wants and pray for us. Great theologians have debated this matter—Aquinas on one side, Bellarmine and St. Alphonsus on the other—but it remains a point on which every Christian must make up his own mind. It is of faith that we can pray for the dead and that they benefit from our prayers; but the suggestion found in so many little devotional manuals that the dead cannot reciprocate is opinion only. If it were true, does it not make a kind of nonsense of continuity? Is it not almost a denial of the reality of purgatory, if to-day my father and I, both living, may pray for each other, while to-morrow, my father being dead, I may continue to pray for him, but he may not pray for me? And here, in the *Memento etiam*, the most pregnant of all moments of prayer for the dead, while we intercede for our beloved, nearer to Christ than we are because made purer than we are, dare we say that they, knowing, are not also praying for us?

(ii) "*The Sign of Faith*"

"The sign of faith" is the indelible mark of baptism. Pictorially, the great vision of the Apocalypse, evoked first in the *Supplices*, still lies behind the words—the sealing of the faithful, so that when the terror and the trial are over, "there shall be no more curse; but the throne of God and of the Lamb shall be in it; and his servants shall serve him: and they shall see his face: and his name shall be in their foreheads." So, praying for the Church Expectant, the Christian dead we see as one with us, a great company, picked out from others by the badge of baptism. The simplicity and directness of the picture matches the simplicity and directness of the definition of a Christian as one who is baptised in the name of the Father and of the Son and of the Holy Ghost. A man may be a good Christian or a bad Christian, a lapsed Christian or a practising Christian; only, if he is baptised, he cannot un-Christ himself and unless he is baptised, he cannot claim the name.

" Unless a man be born again of water and the Holy Ghost," said Jesus, " he cannot enter into the Kingdom of God " and His last command to His disciples was " Go ye, therefore, and teach all nations, baptizing them in the name of the Father and of the Son and of the Holy Ghost." By baptism, which purges from all sin, we become identified with the death on Calvary. " Know ye not," says St. Paul, " that so many of us as were baptized into Jesus Christ were baptized into his death? Therefore we are buried with him by baptism into death: that like as Christ was raised up from the dead by the glory of the Father, even so we also should walk in newness of life. For if we have been planted together in the likeness of his death, we shall be also in the likeness of his resurrection: knowing this, that our old man is crucified with him, that the body of sin might be destroyed, that henceforth we should not serve sin."

The command and its interpretation, compressed into the words of the Creed, " I acknowledge one baptism for the remission of sins," form the basis of a theology which sometimes puzzles the simple by its apparent elaboration. But theology consists of the answers to questions people have asked and in this matter the first and obvious question of any enquirer into the Christian Faith is: If baptism is, in the eyes of Christians, essential, what happens when there is no authorised person available to baptise? To this the Church's answer is that " baptism may be administered by anyone who has sufficient use of reason, catholic or non-catholic, baptized or not." To put it in an extreme theoretical form, a Mohammedan woman may validly baptize a Christian. From this principle arise many other considerations, safeguards, priorities of which one at least is of overwhelming importance to all who pray for unity:—through baptism, that unity does already exist. The question of the ' validity of orders ' which separates Christians on other issues has no application here, for all who have been baptized, by whatever minister, are all equally indelibly signed with " the sign of faith." And no Mass is or has been said, throughout all the world and all the centuries, when prayer has not been made for them, as the church, by the Church.

At the end of the *Memento etiam* the priest bows his head. This is a gesture unparalleled in the Liturgy; nor is there any accepted explanation of it. Many think that it is connected with the fact that Christ on the Cross bowed his head when He died and that the reminiscence is appropriate in a prayer for the dead. It may be so. But the appropriateness is surely carried through to the thought of the baptism, which is our common sharing of his death.

THE NOBIS QUOQUE PECCATORIBUS

To us sinners also, Thy servants, trusting in the multitude of Thy
mercies, vouchsafe to grant some part and fellowship with Thy
holy Apostles and Martyrs: with John, Stephen, Matthias, Barnabas, Ignatius, Alexander, Marcellinus, Peter, Felicity, Perpetua,
Agatha, Lucy, Agnes, Cecilia, Anastasia, and with all Thy Saints,
within whose fellowship we beseech Thee to admit us, not
weighing our merit, but pardoning our offences, through Christ
our Lord.

Nobis quoque peccatoribus famulis tuis, de multitudine miserationum tuarum sperantibus, partem aliquam, et societatem donare
digneris, cum tuis sanctis Apostolis, et Martyribus: cum Joanne,
Stephano, Matthia, Barnaba, Ignatio, Alexandro, Marcellino,
Petro, Felicitate, Perpetua, Agatha, Lucia, Agnete, Caecilia,
Anastasia, et omnibus Sanctis tuis: intra quorum nos consortium,
non aestimator meriti, sed veniae, quaesumus, largitor admitte,
per Christum Dominum nostrum.

(i) The Prayer for the Clergy

THE CLIMATE of the other world continues as the celebrant,
smiting his breast in contrition, prays that we may be
made worthy of the communion of saints. Though, here as
always, the whole congregation is included in the ' we,' the
Nobis quoque peccatoribus was, in the first place, a specific
prayer for the ministers at the altar; and ritually there is still
a relic of that meaning because here—for the only time in

the Canon—the celebrant's voice is audible. The words
' Nobis quoque peccatoribus '—' to us sinners also '—are said
aloud and the celebrant is really speaking to the other priests,
deacons and subdeacons within hearing. Originally this was
the moment when the subdeacons, who had been bowing
since the beginning of the *Preface*, stood erect and left their
positions to prepare the vessels for the Communion of the
Faithful. As the moment of Communion draws nearer, so
the sense of unworthiness deepens in those who are receiving
and dispensing it.

Conscious on the one hand of the immensity of their office
and on the other of the unworthiness of their persons, they
pray that they too may share in the heavenly grace for which,
in the *Supplices*, they have already petitioned in the name of
all. Later, in his private prayer before communicating, the
celebrant himself will utter those words without which it
would be almost impossible to celebrate: " Regard not my
sins, but the faith of Thy Church." And it is some such
prayer which should be in the heart of the laity *for* the priesthood at this moment.

The important thing about a priest is that he does not choose
to be so, but is chosen. " Ye have not chosen me " said Jesus
to the disciples at the Last Supper, " but I have chosen you
and ordained you that ye should go and bring forth fruit."
Once the priesthood is regarded in the light of a ' career '
instead of a vocation, something determined instead of something accepted, every kind of disorder and treachery follows.
All ' anti-clericalism ' is an expression of this disorder, for
which the responsibility sometimes lies with unworthy priests
but is, not less often, due to misunderstandings among laymen.

If we hear the cry " No man shall come between my soul and God," we should answer not by an attempted intellectual argument on the inescapability of intermediaries (such as, for example, the artist) but by an immediate statement of Catholic doctrine,—that between God and his Creation there is only one Priest and he is Jesus Christ. His priesthood is unique; there is no other and all priests are priests only because, by His choice, they share in it. Christ, it has been finely put by Father Alan Keenan, " is the Infinite Worshipper of God in the finite vestments of His humanity "; and for the perpetuation of this worship where alone it is still offered on earth—in the Eucharist—he needs a voice to speak and hands to dispense. That is all that a priest is—the human organism which Christ uses in the Mass for the offering of his sacrifice. Priests have no other essential function but this—to consecrate bread and wine so that they become Christ's Body and Blood, to offer Christ thus present on the altar, to the Father, to communicate Christ thus present to the faithful so as to *make* ' the holy common people of God '—the ' plebs tua sancta ' of the *Unde et memores*. All other functions of the priesthood are allied to or derived from this.

But because, in the world's eyes, the secondary things are often the more prominent—because this priest has a more ' pleasant personality ' than that or that a keener brain than this; because one has ' the common touch ' and another is an ascetical recluse; because Father X is devoted to the souls in a slum-parish and Father Y is a fashionable preacher and Father Z takes his place in sociological and political move ments—because of such surface differences due to the human temperament, men and women sometimes use such trivialities as criteria of 'worthiness.' Yet the idea that any priest is *worthy* of his office rests on a misconception of what he is and what his office is. Between the greatest saint and the greatest scoundrel there is but a hairsbreadth in comparison with the immensity of the gulf between the saint and the one Priest Whose minister he has been called to be. For this reason the Church has always condemned the idea, which in every age rigorist and puritan heresies have fathered, that the private character of the priest can affect the sacrament. To the apparently 'common-sense' remark: " I like to receive my communion from a *good* man," it answers " That you can say that shows that you understand the meaning neither of the Communion nor of goodness."

The priest's acceptance of his total unworthiness has been expressed thus by Father Benson: " The work is wholly His. No skill of man can fashion any work, so that God shall come and approve of it and finish it. He begins and He finishes the work; and so He begins every work in the greatest possible form of weakness. Therefore in all divine works, instead of being discouraged because things seem to be weak, we are to recognize this weakness as an almost necessary form of divine co-operation." That is the basis of Christian humility. The priest's " Lord, I am not worthy " is the admission of every sin and every weakness but one—the unforgivable sin of making 'the great refusal.' And from this springs the 'vast audacity' of this prayer—that our weakness by the mercy of God may be so transformed that we may be made worthy of martyrdom.

This sense of human weakness as a vessel for divine strength is, of course, a distinguishing mark of the faith. St. Paul gave

it its classic expression when he wrote to the self-sure
Corinthians: "If I needs must glory, I will glory of the
things which concern mine infirmities. The God and Father
of our Lord Jesus Christ, which is blessed for ever more,
knoweth that I lie not . . . And he said unto me, My grace is
sufficient for thee, for my strength is made perfect in weakness. Most gladly therefore will I rather glory in my infirmities
that the power of Christ may rest upon me." And, earlier,
to the same Church, he had penned that passage which is the
true comment on Christ's "I have chosen you "—" For ye
see your calling, brethren, how that not many wise men after
the flesh, not many mighty, not many noble, are called: but
God hath chosen the foolish things of the world to confound
the wise; and God hath chosen the weak things of the world
to confound the things that are mighty; and the base things
of the world, and things which are despised, hath God chosen,
yea, and things which are not, to bring to nought things that
are: that no flesh should glory in his presence."

In a world which admires Stoicism and in the country
which gave birth to Pelagianism—that old British heresy
which might even be called modern British orthodoxy and
whose creed has been popularly summed up in Rudyard
Kipling's poem, If—this aspect of the Faith is not always
stressed. But this prayer, which was the work of Pope
Symmachus at the end of that fifth century which saw the
Church's struggle against the self-sufficiency of Pelagianism,
emphasises it beyond escape. The names of the women
martyrs shout it—and, in one at least, who was put to death
by the Stoic hero, Marcus Aurelius, the issue is made explicit
—and the close, "not weighing our merit" (which is

negligible) "but pardoning our offences" (which are innumerable) reiterates the plea of the opening "to us sinners,
also . . ."

(ii) *The Forerunner and the Proto-Martyr*

At the head of the second list of saints in the Canon,
balancing and complementing that in the *Communicantes*,
stands John the Baptist. The mere mention of the forerunner,—the emaciated figure of the desert, clad in skins and
living on locusts and honey; the victim of a king's concubine
and her daughter, Salome, who took his head as a trophy,—
calls up to the imagination one of the great personalities of the
New Testament whose fame has been perpetuated in literature
and art and music. That familiarity is an obstacle to understanding and we must lose that image if we are to find his
significance in the prayer. For here his name epitomizes
exactly those implications of the priesthood which we have
been considering.

John the Baptist is the exemplar of anonymity. In everything he says and does is the consciousness that he is nothing
but the chosen instrument of Christ's glorification. He even
disclaims personality. Asked who he is, he replies ' a voice.'
He is a voice announcing the advent of another; a hand,
pointing to the appearance of another. "He that cometh
after me is preferred before me " . . . "One mightier than I
cometh, the latchet of whose shoes I am not worthy to
unloose."

He does not even arrogate to himself the rôle of a herald,
proclaiming in the capital the coming of the king. He retires

obscurely to the desert, content to preach repentance to any who care to come to him. When Jesus presents himself for baptism, he shrinks from performing it: " I have need to be baptized of thee, and comest *thou* to *me*? " But the same humility which makes him hesitate also makes him obey as soon as Jesus insists: " Suffer it to be so now, for thus it becometh us to fulfil all righteousness."

In the Baptist, St. Augustine discerned clearly enough the true type of priestly service. In one of his sermons he used him as an example to those who, even in those early years of Christianity, had a wrong and arrogating conception of their custodianship of the sacraments. " Ye ought to note, holy brethren, if John so humbled himself as to say ' I am not worthy to unloose His shoe's latchet,' how they require to be humbled who say ' *We* baptize; what *we* give is ours and ours is holy.' John saith, ' not I, but He '; they say, ' We.' John is not unworthy to unloose His shoe's latchet: but if he had said he was worthy, expressing himself thus: ' He cometh after me who is made before me, of whom I am but worthy to unloose the shoe's latchet,' even this had been a great humbling of himself. But, when he speaks of his worthiness as not reaching even thus far, full indeed must he have been of the Holy Spirit, who did thus as a servant acknowledge his Lord, and of a servant merited to be made a friend."

Above all, it was John who first said those words which every priest at every Mass repeats: " Behold the Lamb of God That taketh away the sins of the world."

Following John comes Stephen, the Proto-Martyr of the Church, at whose stoning Saul the persecutor presided. His eminence, as the first of all the noble army of martyrs, has eclipsed the lowliness of his status in the Church during his lifetime. As the number of converts increased during the first days of the apostles' preaching in Jerusalem, so the practical details of organisation, especially in looking after the poor, took up more and more of their time. So the Twelve called the members of the Church together and said: "It is not reason that we should leave the word of God and serve tables; wherefore, brethren, look ye out among you seven men of honest report, full of the Holy Ghost and wisdom, whom we may appoint over this business." Thus were the deacons chosen, among whom was Stephen.

He, neither priest nor apostle, is chosen as the first to witness with his blood for Christ, according to that mysterious precedence which is not of human appointment; and, as if conscious of the singularity of the honour, gives to after-ages the precedent of an humble obedience to his Lord, in dying with forgiveness on his lips: "Lord, lay not this sin to their charge."

(iii) *Matthias and Barnabas*

The anonymity of Matthias and the self-effacement of Barnabas reinforce the example of John and Stephen. Of Matthias we know nothing beyond the bare record in the *Acts of the Apostles*. Almost immediately after the Ascension, Peter addressed the hundred and twenty followers of Christ in Jerusalem and pointed out that it was necessary to fill the place of the traitor, Judas, who had committed suicide. "'Wherefore of these men which have companied with us all the time that the Lord Jesus went in and out among us, beginning from the baptism of John unto the same day that he was taken up from us,' he said, ' must one be ordained to be a witness with us of his resurrection.'

" And they appointed two, Joseph called Barnabas, who was surnamed Justus, and Matthias. And they prayed and said ' Thou, Lord, which knowest the hearts of all men, show whether of these two thou hast chosen, that he may take part of this ministry and apostleship, from which Judas by transgression fell, that he might go to his own place.' And they gave forth their lots; and the lot fell upon Matthias; and he was numbered with the eleven apostles."

That is all. No deed, no word spoken by Matthias survives. Even traditions of his ministry and martyrdom are so contradictory that they must be accounted as confusions with another Matthias who was Bishop of Jerusalem about 120 or with the apocryphal *Gospel of Matthias*. The abasement of the thirteenth apostle is absolute. Even here in the Canon he is not given his place with the eleven; St. Paul fills that, as he does in the thought of the Church and in the regard of history. By the side of the great ' Apostle of the Gentiles ' the substitute for Judas dwarfs into insignificance. Moreover, because Matthias was chosen before the Holy Ghost was given at Pentecost, the method of his election was what an unconvinced onlooker might have described as chance. Though the fall of the dice was on this unique occasion controlled by God in answer to prayer, a certain unexpressed scepticism— human nature being what it is—cannot be ruled out among the supporters of the rival candidate. Nor—again on the human level—can the thought of the former holder of his office have been altogether banished from Matthias's mind.

And in the lack of any record or acknowledgment of him whatever, in contrast to the other candidate of whom we do at least know that he was called 'the Just,' may we not infer a certain atmosphere of indifference among his contemporaries? One thing only is clear—that Matthias was chosen. And his name bears witness that that one thing only is of consequence.

'Barnabas' was a nickname meaning 'the son of Consolation' given to a Cypriot named Joses. His anonymity is of a different kind from Matthias's—sought rather than imposed. Of his actions and his life we do indeed know something; though of his background, his origin and his fate, nothing. He enters the story of the early Church and leaves it with a charity and a self-effacement which has led some to describe him as ' the great gentleman.' That he was of imposing appearance is deduced from the fact that by the pagan inhabitants of Lystra he was acclaimed as Jupiter; that he was a man of means, by his selling his property in Jerusalem and giving the proceeds to the common purse of the first Christians; that he was well regarded by them, because it was on his word, and his alone, that the apostles consented to see their mortal enemy Saul the persecutor after his conversion. They naturally had doubts about its genuineness; the announcement of it might have been a trick to gain access to them and to exterminate the Church in Jerusalem. But they accepted Barnabas's guarantee and thus ' the Son of Consolation ' was instrumental in saving Paul for the Church, for the first time. He saved him the second time when, at his suggestion, Paul's long exile in Tarsus (where Peter and James for safety's sake had sent him) was brought to an end by the choice of him to preach the gospel at Antioch. Barnabas not only initiated the policy, but journeyed to Paul with the news and stayed with him as fellow-worker, both in Antioch and on the ' first missionary journey.' With that, his work for Paul was done. ' Barnabas and Paul ' became ' Paul and Barnabas ' and then ' Paul,' while Barnabas went to the protection of another—the John Mark who wrote the Gospel of Mark and who was his nephew. On the first missionary journey, young Mark had turned back; when, during the planning of the second, Barnabas suggested taking him again, Paul refused to have him. Barnabas characteristically gave the protection of his loyalty to the younger and weaker man and took Mark with him to Cyprus, leaving Paul to find another travelling-companion. And with this gesture, Barnabas disappears from history, as self-effacing in his exit as in his entrance.

(iv) Ignatius of Antioch

When at the end of one of their journeys Jesus and his disciples had arrived at Capernaum, " He asked them, What was it that ye disputed among yourselves by the way? But they held their peace: for by the way they had disputed among themselves who should be the greatest. And he sat down and called the twelve and saith unto them, If any man desire to be first, the same shall be last of all and servant of all. And he took a child and set him in the midst of them: and when he had taken him in his arms, he said unto them, Whosoever shall receive one of such children in my name, receiveth me." So Mark records the episode; and Matthew adds that Jesus pointed the occasion by saying " Whosoever shall humble himself as this little child, the same is greatest in the Kingdom of Heaven."

The child who was thus held up as the example of Christian humility was, by some writers of the early Church, said to be Ignatius. This sacred legend is chronologically possible, and, if it were true, Ignatius's age would have been about seventy-seven when, as Bishop of Antioch, he was thrown to the beasts in one of Trajan's gladiatorial spectacles in Rome in the October of A.D. 107. What is certain is that Ignatius was a pupil of the Apostles and that he was ordained Bishop of Antioch by Peter himself: that on his way to martyrdom he wrote at least seven letters which are among the cardinal documents of the Christian church (he refers, for instance, to the ' Eucharist ' by that name as well as to ' the Catholic Church '); and that because of his impassioned cry for martyrdom in his letter to the Romans—a cry which, in Dean Farrar's phrase, " marks a new epoch in the history of the world "—he has been given the title of ' the master of martyrdom.'

Ignatius enters history as a man doomed to die. Condemned at Antioch for refusing to sacrifice to the pagan gods, he was reserved for death in Rome as a spectacle for the populace. The decision may have been a personal one—an attempt to terrify the Christians in Rome by exhibiting the fate of one so eminent among them,—but it is more probable that Ignatius was merely a ' routine item ' of the regulation by which provincial governors had to provide criminals for the insatiable blood-lust which the capital slaked in the amphitheatre.[1] He

[1] In his games in 106—the year before Ignatius's martyrdom—Trajan provided 10,000 gladiators alone.

was sent guarded by ten soldiers under conditions which were themselves a little martyrdom. "From Syria to Rome," he wrote, "I fight with wild beasts, by land and sea, by night and by day, being bound amidst ten leopards, even a company of soldiers, who only wax worse when they are kindly treated." Yet the journey was a kind of triumph. News of his fate had preceded him and, at the cities through which he passed, the Christian communities came to him giving encouragement, asking blessing. At the outset, some influential friends had hurried direct to Rome to try to organize there a petition for his release. And it is to the Roman Christians, forbidding them to take steps on his behalf, that Ignatius wrote his immortal letter.

"If you keep silence about me, I shall become a 'word' of God; but if you love my flesh too much, I shall again be a mere 'sound.' Grant me nothing more than that I may be poured out as a libation to God while the altar is still prepared. I bid all men know that of my own free will I die for God, unless you hinder me. I implore you, be not an 'unseasonable kindness' to me. I am God's wheat to be ground by the teeth of beasts to become Christ's pure bread. Agree with me. I know what is good for me. Now I begin to be a disciple. My birthday is at hand. Suffer me to come to the pure light; when I reach it I shall be a man indeed. Of what value is all the world? Better to die for Christ than to rule over its farthest kingdoms. Suffer me to imitate the passion of my God. Earthly love (eros) has been crucified in me and there is no longer fire of love for material things; but only a living water that speaks to me within my soul, Come to the Father. I write to you in the midst of life, yet lusting after death. You will only be showing envy and hatred towards me, not love, if you procure the saving of my life."

His wish was granted and he died—to use one of his characteristic phrases from his last letter to his friend Polycarp, Bishop of Smyrna " steadfast as a smitten anvil."

(v) Alexander, Marcellinus, Peter

The names of Marcellinus and Peter take us to the last of the great persecutions, that of Diocletian, which reached its peak in the year 304 when every Christian throughout the Empire was presented with the choice between adoration of the Emperor or death by torture. Only in the provinces of Gaul and Britain was there a certain laxity of enforcement, though even here it produced our proto-martyr, St. Alban. Elsewhere the Empire ' ran with the blood of Christians.' The very fierceness and unexpectedness of the attack—unexpected, because both Diocletian's wife and daughter were catechumens —invited apostasy; and many Christians in high places handed over the sacred Scriptures and liturgical books to destruction in an effort to save their lives. Thus not only the bodies of Christians but the records of the Faith were destroyed by a state which had determined to root Christianity out not only by persecution but by propaganda. Having destroyed practically every Christian writing, it prepared a blasphemous *Acts of Pilate* which was ordered to be learnt by heart in all the schools.

At such a moment, Rome itself should have been a rock, and the Pope, Marcellinus, have shown himself a worthy successor of St. Peter. But he seems momentarily to have apostasised. The details are confused and though later writings suggest that the contemporary accusation that he actually sacrificed to the gods was untrue, he was certainly guilty of some temporary weakness and his name was for long omitted from the list of the Popes. In any case, as Duchesne remarks, " for a personage of such importance it was regrettable enough in such a time to die in his bed."

But he had a namesake, a priest named Marcellinus, attached to whose church was Peter, an exorcist.[1] Peter, imprisoned as a Christian, converted his gaoler and all his family and brought them to Marcellinus to be baptized. The inevitable result was that both priest and exorcist were martyred with some ferocity.

These two simple obscure men had, as it transpired, a unique honour. In this fiercest of the persecutions, they were the only Roman clerics who died for their faith. On their shoulders rested the honour of the priesthood of Rome. " The Roman bishop and the other members of the higher clergy, except the above clerics," says the *Catholic Encyclopaedia* in writing of them, " were able to elude the persecutors. How this happened we do not know. It is possible that Pope Marcellinus was able to hide himself in a safe place of concealment in due time, as many other bishops did. But it is also possible that at the publication of the edict he secured his own immunity."

But if the Pope temporised, his namesake died—and Rome remembered. For the cemetery of Ss. Peter and Marcellinus, where the martyrs were buried and, when peace returned, publicly honoured, was also known quite simply as ' ad duos

---

[1] An exorcist, one of the minor orders of the Church, was usually in charge of the catechumens who, still being in a state of original sin, were liable to diabolic attacks. One of the chief duties of an exorcist was to take part in baptismal exorcism.

lauros '—' the two victors.' And when five hundred years later, the biographer of Charlemagne turned monk and founded a Benedictine abbey in his estates in Germany, the saints whose relics he coveted above all were those of Marcellinus and Peter, which lie now, not in their cemetery in Rome but at Seligenstadt, so named in their honour.

The identity of Alexander is unknown. There are many Alexanders among the early martyrs, and liturgiologists disagree as to which of them is intended here. The general opinion is either the Alexander who was the seventh son of St. Felicity or the first Pope of that name, who followed the Clement mentioned in the earlier list. He, the fifth Pope, (martyred in the year A.D. 113), would have a particular relevance to the dominating thought of the prayer, for by his order, water was added to the wine of the chalice and the symbolism of this water has come to express with exactitude the burden of this thought.

The water is the symbol of our own weak humanity. When it is poured into the chalice at the Offertory it is now accompanied by one of the most perfect prayers of the Mass, the adaptation of an old Roman Christmas Collect: " O God Who didst wonderfully create and yet more wonderfully renew the dignity of the human nature, grant that by the mystery of this water and wine we may be made partakers of His divinity Who vouchsafed to share our humanity." And, though this use of the prayer is comparatively late, the connotation of the water is not; and in the very earliest days, when the faithful brought their offerings to the Eucharist, it was the poor orphans, who had nothing of their own to bring, who were the water-bearers.

It would indeed be appropriate if the St. Alexander to whom we owe this rite and of whom nothing else but his service and his martyrdom are known, were the saint of the prayer; though one would not wish to exclude the other Alexander who was the youngest son of the saint who heads the seven women-martyrs who follow.

(vi) Felicity and Perpetua

Felicity stands for all time the type of Christian, as opposed to Stoic, courage—the admitted weakness that knows that God will make strong. Her memorable words, indeed, epitomise the whole matter. She was one of the Carthaginian martyrs of the year 203 who, with Perpetua and Perpetua's brother and others, was thrown to the beasts in the amphitheatre at Carthage. A detailed account of their arrest, imprisonment and death survives, which is undoubtedly authentic and part of which was written by Perpetua herself; and when, in 1907, the excavators were at work in Carthage, the memorial stone, inscribed with their names, was discovered.

" As for Felicity," records the account of their Passion, " she received this grace from the Lord. Because she was now gone eight months (she was indeed with child when she was arrested) she sorrowed greatly as the day of the games drew near, fearing lest for this reason she should be kept back and shed her innocent blood after the rest, among strangers and evil-doers. Also her fellow-martyrs were much disturbed lest they should leave behind them so good a friend who was, as it were, a fellow-traveller on the road of the same hope.

So, with united fervour they made their prayer to God, three days before the games. Immediately after their prayer, her pains came on her. And when, because of the natural difficulty of the eighth month, she was oppressed by her travail and cried out grievously, one of the guards said to her ' You that are now crying out, what will you do when you are thrown to the beasts, which you made light of when you would not sacrifice?' And she answered, ' What I suffer now, I suffer myself: but then Another shall be in me who shall suffer for me, because I shall suffer for Him.' " And so, " on the day of their victory," " Felicity, rejoicing that she had borne a child in safety, that she might fight with the beasts, came now from blood to blood, from the midwife to the gladiator, to wash after her travail in a second baptism."

Felicity was a slave, the mother of several children. Perpetua was an aristocrat of twenty-two. Her individuality is recognisable enough, seventeen centuries after. When the women came to the entrance of the arena, they were given the dress of the priestesses of Ceres to put on. Perpetua refused and said to her guards: " We are dying because we will do no such thing: this was our bargain with you." She insisted that the objection was taken to the tribune, with the result that they were allowed " to be brought forth as they were, without more ado." When they came into the open arena, they pointed to the president of the games, the deputy of the Emperor, and called: " Thou judgest us and God thee," which enraged the people to such an extent that the mob demanded their scourging. " Then truly they gave thanks because they had received something of the sufferings of the Lord Jesus."

" For the women the Devil had made ready a most savage
cow, prepared for this purpose against all custom; for even
in this beast he would make mock of their sex. They were
stripped and made to wear nets. The people shuddered, seeing
one a tender girl, the other her breasts still dropping from her
childbearing. So they were called back and given loose robes
to wear. Perpetua was first thrown. When she sat up, as her
robe was torn, she drew it over to cover her thigh, mindful
of modesty rather than pain. Next, looking for a pin, she
pinned up her dishevelled hair, saying that it was unseemly
that a Christian should suffer with her hair dishevelled, lest
she should appear to be grieving in her glory. So she stood
up." In the end, she died by beheading and "when the
swordsman's hand wandered (for he was a novice), she herself
set it upon her own neck." The eyewitness who wrote the
account of the final scene concludes: "Perhaps so great a
woman could not else have been killed (being feared by the
Evil Spirit) had she not herself so willed it."

(vii) *Agatha, Lucy, Agnes, Cecilia, Anastasia*

Compared with Felicity and Perpetua, the remaining five
martyrs are shadowy figures whose identity tends to be
obscured by the great growth of legends about them. Yet, as
these stories are so much part of the devotional piety of the
common people and, through their constant representation in
the art of Christendom, have passed into the currency of
civilization, it would be wrong to ignore them altogether.
Also, it would be foolish; for the probability is that all are
founded on a basis of truth.

Agatha was martyred in Sicily in the Decian persecution of 251 and from that moment the veneration of her never ceased. In Rome, at the time of Gregory the Great, a great church in her honour had been standing for over a century. During the Gothic invasions it had been desecrated and it was Gregory himself who reconsecrated it for Catholic worship and attached to it a school of deacons. In the same century the *Acts* of St. Agatha (which are ' legendary ') were compiled—a distance of time equal to that between our own days and those of Sir Christopher Wren—and references to St. Agatha made in the great christian poems of Venantius Fortunatus. There seems no good reason therefore for rejecting the story that, in an attempt to force Agatha to renounce her vow of virginity, the Roman Governor ordered her breasts to be cut off and that she rebuked him with: " Cruel tyrant, are you not ashamed to wound in a woman the breast you sucked in your mother? ", nor for dismissing as apocryphal the reference to Christ's parable of the house built upon the rock which inspired her answer to his threats: " My courage and my mind are so firmly founded upon the rock of my Lord Jesus Christ that no assault can move me: your words are but wind, your promises are but rain, your menaces are passing floods and however hardly these things hurtle at the foundation of my courage, they cannot change me."

Thirty years after Agatha's martyrdom at Catania, Lucy was born in Syracuse, about fifty miles away. Her father died when she was a child and she was brought up by her mother Eutychia. The girl, deciding to take a vow of poverty and virginity, wished to distribute all her inherited wealth among the poor. But Eutychia forbade it until, herself making a pilgrimage to Agatha's tomb, she was cured of a hæmorrhage from which she had been suffering for several years. Thereupon in gratitude she fell in with the wishes of her daughter and together they gave away to charitable purposes the greater part of their money and property. This action so infuriated the young man who was officially betrothed to Lucy that he denounced her as a Christian to the governor of Sicily. The year was that 303 which saw the outbreak of the last and most bitter phase of the Diocletian persecution. As Lucy refused to recant, she was put to death by the sword.

Of these two Sicilian martyrs, both to become so famous in Rome, it was Lucy who became the more popular in England, because of the devotion to her of St. Aldhelm, the famous Saxon Abbot of Malmesbury. He was the first to write her life in full and, copying him, the Venerable Bede inserted it in his Martyrology.

Another victim of the Diocletian persecution was the thirteen-year-old Agnes, for whom, when she was arrested, ' no fetters could be found small enough for her wrists.' She was the daughter of wealthy parents and her hand was sought in marriage by the son of the Prefect of Rome. It was in refusing his suit that she betrayed herself, for she told him she was already espoused to a bridegroom nobler than any on earth, who had betrothed her by the ring of his faith and would crown her with jewels to which earthly gifts were as dross. Realising that she was a Christian, he denounced her to his father and, refusing to recant, she was executed after having been sent to a brothel, where, naked, she said quietly: " I have His angel, who is the keeper of my body " and, her long hair veiling her, none dared touch her. The Prefect's son—it was said—who came to her last of all, fell senseless before her and was restored only by her prayers.

Agnes's youth and her "double martyrdom, one of modesty, the other of religion " (as St. Ambrose put it) made an immediate and lasting impression on the imagination of Christians. Within fifty years of her death, a church was erected by Constantine's order, over her tomb in a garden a mile from the city; and another—one of the most beautiful of all Roman churches—on the site of the brothel. At the former every year still on the anniversary of her martyrdom, January 21, two lambs are blessed—emblems of innocence and of her name—from whose wool are woven the pallia which the pope presents to Archbishops. The pallium recalls to its wearer the obligation of bearing on the neck, like the Good Shepherd, the sick and strayed sheep; and it is fitting that this, which is also the symbol of the highest ecclesiastical authority (for, in the early centuries, it was worn by the Pope alone), should be for ever associated with the child martyr who, in the words of Pope Damasus inscribed on her tomb, ' overcame her intense fear with her feeble strength.'

Cecilia suffered under Marcus Aurelius in the year 117. This fact is perhaps the most important aspect, for us to-day, of the inclusion of her name. During the nineteenth century, a growing admiration for the Stoic author of the *Meditations*, which became a Victorian bedside-book, combined with a liberal and humanist imprecision as to the meaning of the Faith, led to a confusion of values. Cecilia was a legendary figure, a patroness of music,[1] met with in literature and art;

---

[1] Cecilia has no connection with music. Her patronage rests on a misunderstanding of an antiphon in her Office.—*antantibus organis Cecilia Domino decantabat*—" which means that while the *pagans* played their instruments, Cecilia sang hymns to God."

Marcus Aurelius was a great and good man, even, as one biography of him put it, 'Saviour of Men.' But their confrontation is a reminder that, for the Christian, Marcus Aurelius stands with Nero; perhaps even a little lower than Nero, since he knew enough of Christianity to reject it and to counsel men to face death " not in sheer obstinacy, like the Christians."

The 'legend' of St. Cecilia is that, on refusing to deny the Christianity in which she had been brought up, she was condemned to be suffocated in her own bath. As before she was taken prisoner she had arranged that her house should be given to the Roman Christians for use as a church, the building after her death became doubly venerable. In the barbarian invasions it was destroyed, to be rebuilt in the ninth century when also St. Cecilia's body was found, with a bloodstained napkin at the feet. In the sixteenth century, the sarcophagus was again opened and Cecilia was seen by many notable witnesses, lying peacefully on her side, as if asleep.

Cecilia became looked upon as the protectress of a Rome which owed to Marcus Aurelius nothing but an acceleration of its decadence; and this aspect of her lives in the Liturgy, not on her own feast in November, but for the Mass for the Wednesday in the second week in Lent, when in Rome the Pope himself used to offer the Holy Sacrifice at her altar-tomb. The Epistle for this day, chosen with care, is from the book of Esther—the prayer of Mordecai for the protection of his people: " Have mercy on thy people because our enemies have resolved to destroy us " which was answered through the instrumentality of Esther, a foretype of the Christian saint.

Last of all comes Anastasia, whose name means ' Resurrection.' All that is known of her is that she suffered for the Faith at Sirmium[1] in the Diocletian persecution and that she is said to have been a pupil of that Chrysogonus whose name appears in the *Communicantes* list of saints. Thus in complete anonymity the procession of martyrs ends. Yet Anastasia has her own peculiar and unique honour. She suffered on Christmas day and because of this her commemoration is at the dawn Mass of the nativity. Originally, it was only that— a Mass celebrated not in honour of the birth of Christ (that had been done at midnight) but in remembrance of this martyred Greek girl. It was said at dawn because of her name and the hour of the resurrection. Eventually that circumstance led to the present custom of the celebration of the three different Masses on December 25, so that it may be said that in a unique way there fell to Anastasia the honour of increasing the honour paid to him for whom she suffered.

[1] Mitrowitz in Jugoslavia.

THE PER QUEM HAEC OMNIA

By whom, O Lord, all these good things Thou dost ever create, sanctify, quicken, bless and bestow on us.

Per quem haec omnia, Domine, semper bona creas, sanctificas, vivificas, benedicis, et praestas nobis.

(i) "All these good things"

THE LAST prayer ended with a comma, ". . . through Christ our Lord," and leads immediately into the great Doxology, which starts with a reference to 'all these good things.'

What are they? The immediate reference, of course, is to the Body and Blood now on the altar about to be liturgically offered to the Father; but these include everything in the orders of nature and grace; everything that has ever been made, " received in their very source under the figure of the consecrated elements designated by a triple sign of the Cross."

But there is also in the words the reminder of a lost particularity. In the earliest days at this point in the Mass, between the last words of the *Nobis quoque peccatoribus* and the first of this prayer, anything which required blessing was brought to the altar and, in a short prayer (of which only the 'through Christ our Lord' remains), was solemnly blessed. Some think that the threefold Cross now made here over the Body and Blood was the gesture originally connected with that blessing. Though the custom has fallen into desuetude, it is worth reviving the memory of it as we pray this prayer, because it illumines the mind of the early Church.

Cardinal Bona, the gentle seventeenth century scholar whose monumental history of the Mass took seven years to write, has said of it that " the religious sense of our ancestors was such that they required all sacred and ecclesiastical ceremonies, the administration of the Sacraments and all blessings, to take place at the Holy Sacrifice, because they understood how the holy Eucharist perfected and completed them. Whether it was the signing of a treaty, a reconciliation, the offering of some gift to God, the proclamation of the feasts of saints, the imposition of a fast; were there litanies to be said, penitents to be reconciled, virgins to be dedicated, priests to be ordained, bishops to be consecrated, kings to be crowned or the holy chrism to be made; all such things, Christians of earlier ages believed, could not properly be accomplished without the celebration of Mass. Gradually lukewarmness and slackness separated many of these things from the Eucharist for fear that the Sacrifice should take too long."

So here, at Easter and Pentecost, milk and honey for the the catechumens were blessed; on the Sunday after Easter the lambs of St. Agnes (which were led round the church during the singing of the *Agnus Dei* a few moments later); on Ascension Day, new beans; on the feast of St. Sixtus,[1]

[1] See p. 69

new grapes; and on Maundy Thursday, the holy oils—the one custom which remains, for they are still blessed on that day, and the oil of the sick, which is used for Extreme Unction, at that very point in the Mass.

All the gifts of God are thus, in the Church's thought and intention, brought into the context of the one great Gift, the first-fruits of the new creation, Jesus Christ; and it is right that we should think here of the sanctification of our possessions.

(ii) " Create, sanctify, quicken, bless and bestow "

The words used of them, " create, sanctify, quicken, bless and bestow," might form the basis of many a meditation; for their implications are almost limitless. By Him everything was created—for the Word was in the world from the very beginning; and " all things were made by him and without him was not anything made that was made." By Him they were sanctified—by Him who for the sake of his followers ' sanctified himself.' " Quicken, bless and bestow "—things made alive, kept from harmful purposes and freely given: the reminder that ' every good and every perfect gift comes down from God ': the opposite of the harmful things sold by the world, alive for evil, costing much in misery.

It is this point which, in the circumstances of our world to-day, we might well stress in the prayer. In one sense, it is dictated by a prayer which explicitly brings the things on earth we love back into the orbit of God. As God made the things of matter and as, at the Eucharist, they are taken into the context of his remaking, they are good. They cannot be otherwise. But in the world outside, they are turned to evil in the hands of the diabolic forces, acting through men. Long ago Augustine defined the diabolic as 'knowledge without charity'—a definition which, with the advance of 'science' (which is exactly that) seems relevant as never before. For once the world has refused to obey the Church and to acknowledge her as the final arbiter of what is and what is not lawful to know and to do, "all these good things" become instruments of harm as we are seeing, with selfish terror, to-day.

Newman in those sermons on Antichrist, preached in 1838, from which I have already quoted, has a strangely prophetic passage which is based, not on anything which he saw round him, but from a study of the Bible and the Fathers. He is speaking of the circumstances of the last persecution. "The reign of Antichrist will be supported, it would appear, by a display of miracles such as the magicians of Egypt effected against Moses. On this subject, of course, we wait for a fuller explanation of the prophetical language such as the event alone can give us. So far, however, it is clear that, whether real miracles or not, whether pretended, or the result, as some have conjectured, of discoveries in physical science, they will produce the same effect as if they were real, namely the overpowering of the imaginations of such as have not the love of God deeply lodged in their hearts—of all but the elect. Scripture is remarkably precise and consistent in this prediction. 'Signs and wonders,' says our Lord, 'insomuch that if it were possible they shall deceive the very elect.' St. Paul speaks of Antichrist as one 'whose coming is after the working of Satan, with all power and signs and lying wonders and with all deceivableness of unrighteousness in them that perish; because they received not the love of Truth, that they might be saved. And for this cause God shall send them strong delusion that they should believe a lie.' And St. John: ' He doeth great wonders, so that he maketh fire come down from heaven on the earth in the sight of men and deceiveth them that dwell on the earth by the means of those miracles which he had power to do in the sight of the Beast.'

" Signs do occur from time to time, not to enable us to fix the day, for that is hidden, but to show us it is coming . . . And surely it is profitable to think about it, though we may be quite mistaken in the detail. For instance, after all it may not be a persecution of blood and death, but of craft and subtilty—not of miracles, but of natural wonders and powers of human skill, human acquirements in the hands of the Devil. Satan may adopt the more alarming weapons of deceit—he may hide himself—he may attempt to seduce us in little things, and so to move the Church, not all at once but by little and little from her true position . . . to split us up and to divide us, to dislodge us gradually off our rock of strength. And if there is to be a persecution, perhaps it will be then; then, perhaps, when we are all of us in all parts of Christendom so divided and so reduced, so full of schism, so close upon heresy. When we have cast ourselves upon the world and depend for protection upon it, and have given up our independence and our strength, then he may burst upon us in fury as far as God allows him. Then suddenly the Roman Empire may break up, and Antichrist appear as a persecutor and the barbarous nations around break in. But all these things are in God's hand and God's knowledge and there let us leave them."

And, it seems to me, in so far as we pray understandingly the *Per quem haec omnia* week by week at Mass, we shall grow in sensitive discrimination of the meaning of the world around us where ' all these good things ' have been desanctified, unblest and appropriated by greed for harm and so, under

> All the easy speeches
> That comfort cruel men,

discern the signs of the times.

THE PER IPSUM

Through Him and with Him and in Him, be unto Thee, O God the Father Almighty, in the unity of the Holy Ghost, all honour and glory, world without end.

Per ipsum et cum ipso et in ipso, est tibi, Deo Patri omnipotenti, in unitate Spiritus Sancti, omnis honor et gloria, per omnia saecula saeculorum.

(i) *The Doxology*

THIS IS the greatest doxology in liturgy, exalting Christ in His character as mediator in language which ' recalls the concentrated rapture of St. Paul's Christology.' It also recalls one of St. Paul's own doxologies in such a way that it constitutes a challenge rather than a reminiscence. A doxology —a short verse praising God and beginning, as a rule, with the Greek word, *doxa*, glory—was both inherited from synagogue worship and borrowed from Greek and Roman rites in honour of the Supreme Being. The Jewish Prayer of Manasses ends with: " I will praise Thee for ever all the days of my life, for all the powers of the heavens do praise Thee and Thine is the glory for ever and ever." And the " for of Him and through Him and unto Him are all things: to Him be glory for ever and ever," which St. Paul uses in reference to God (not to Christ as in the *Per Ipsum*) is identical with a Stoic formula, which is also found incorporated in a hymn to Selene and inscribed on a gem as a charm.

What is unique about this Christian praise is—Christ. The very fact that it is, in its wording, virtually indistinguishable from the formula for the ' Unknown God ' of the Gentiles and the ' Ineffable Name ' of the Jews makes it a challenge. It is *through* Jesus, the only mediator of God and man; *with* Jesus, equal to the Father; *in* Jesus, consubstantial with the Father, that the same God the Father Almighty is honoured and glorified. God cannot be praised in any other way or by any other means. For the Christian, the term ' God ' derives its meaning from Christ.

Further, the doxology is connected in thought with the preceding prayer. The two-fold aspect of Christ is stated paradoxically—which, indeed, is the only way possible. The Gift is the Giver. In the *Per quem*, we remember that all good things descend from God through Christ; in the *Per ipsum* that all glory reascends to God through Christ. That is to say "Jesus is at once God giving himself to man and man giving himself to God, being thus the confluence of the two loves," as Zundel says. " The Canon ends with this encounter in which the mystery of the Cross reveals its depths: God crucified in man and man crucified in God, in the unity of one Person, a Divine Person. What thanksgiving can befit such a Gift, save the Gift Itself? "

Mention has already been made of the gesture which accompanies this prayer—the five-fold sign of the Cross followed by the elevation of Host and Chalice together in a gesture of offering, the remnant of the ancient ceremony in which the celebrant lifted up the consecrated Bread and the deacon the great two-handled Chalice and touched one with the other.[1]

The lifting-up of the Host and Chalice, outward and visible sign of the offering of the Acceptable Sacrifice to God, coincides with the words *omnis honor et gloria*, ' all honour and glory,' so that the symbolism of language and action are fused in one. The gesture is, by a confusion of titles, known as the ' Little Elevation,' in contradistinction to the ' Elevation ' in the *Qui Pridie* when the celebrant lifts above his head for the congregation to see and worship the just-consecrated Host and Chalice. That—the ' Elevation '—is, however, a much later development, which belongs to the great wave of Eucharistic devotion of that thirteenth century in which the Feast of Corpus Christi was instituted.[2] But this ' Little Elevation 'of the *Per Ipsum* is the proper and primitive liturgical elevation; and still, in Belgium and other countries, it is here that the bell is rung to announce the moment of it. " Together with the Consecration, it constitutes one of the solemn acts of the Eucharistic Prayer. In the sacred economy of the Mass— fully entitled to our respect—the Little Elevation is to be venerated as the deepest manifestation of the adorable Trinity and the highest expression of the oblation made to It of Jesus Christ."

Finally, the Per Ipsum may be regarded as a summary of the meaning of the whole action, which is to *give thanks* to God for *His great glory*—that is, as Dom Eugène Vandeur expresses it, " for the glory He possesses in Himself; for that

[1] See pp. 33, 34
[2] Pope Innocent III, for example, who died in 1216, knew nothing of the ' Elevation.'

which is shown forth in His works, especially in the work of the Incarnate Word, the Redeemer; for the merits He has obtained and applied to men. Their salvation effected *through* Jesus Christ, *with* Jesus Christ and *in* Jesus Christ ever gives all honour and glory to God."

(ii) *The Holy Trinity*

The Christian definition of God is continued in the phrase " in the unity of the Holy Ghost." This is the only reference in the Canon to the third person of the Trinity, inseparable from the Father and the Son, co-operater in the divine work. Since the Holy Trinity is the central doctrine of the Christian religion—is, in fact, the revelation about the nature of God which Jesus came to deliver to the world and is, therefore, the foundation of all Christian theology—it is proper that at these words we should recollect something of its immensity. Though beyond our comprehension, it is not beyond our devotion. As a warning to every commentator, indeed, is the vision of St. Augustine who when walking by the sea-shore and wrestling in his mind with the meaning of the doctrine, noticed a child trying to empty the ocean into a hole that it had dug in the sand. Augustine explained to the boy that he was trying to do the impossible. " Not more so," came the reply, " than for you to explain the mystery on which you are meditating."

Yet, because the doctrine which is at the core of the Faith is too often dismissed even by the faithful as an inscrutable technicality, vaguely associated with a mathematical impossibility or a childish analogy drawn from a clover-leaf, some attempt must be made to suggest a mode of meditation which may explain why the phrase ' the Holy and Adorable Trinity ' is not a pious *cliché* but the statement of a fact which modern man desperately needs for his comfort.

The Holy Trinity is a revealed mystery. It is a mystery in the sense in which Gerard Manley Hopkins wrote to one of his non-Christian friends: " By mystery, you mean an interesting uncertainty, but a Catholic means by ' mystery ' an incomprehensible certainty." And it is a truth of revelation in that it cannot be arrived at by the processes of human reasoning, though, once it is ' given,' it both illumines reason and is seen not to be contrary to it. " You must believe in order to understand " is a statement of the inevitable order of priorities. If, in speaking of the Holy Trinity, we are bound to use human analogies, there is no implication that by seeing them we arrive at the doctrine. On the contrary, it is by accepting the doctrine that we see them.

The problem of all living, as of all philosophy, is the relationship of the many and the one—to reduce the multiciplicity of ourselves to an integrity. ' Integrity ' not ' integer.' That is the clue. To think in terms of a *mathematical* unity (if, strictly speaking, such a thing exists) is from the outset to misunderstand how in the unity of the Godhead there are three Persons, the Father, the Son and the Holy Spirit, and these three Persons are truly distinct—or, in the words of the Athanasian Creed " the Father is God, the Son is God and the Holy Spirit is God; yet they are not three Gods but one God."

The concept of unity which makes understanding easier is that of an *organic* unity—or even an *aesthetic* unity. The unity of a picture consists in the right handling and inter-relationship of diverse elements; and the more powerful and individual the separate elements, each in its own right: colour: form: subject: the greater, providing the unity is achieved, the picture will be. A simple formal design in pencil—which is the nearest approach to the mathematical idea of unity—is hardly comparable with one of Tintoretto's masterpieces. In the organic unity of human life, the distance is even greater between the unicellular amoeba (again recalling mathematical unity) and that most many-sided of geniuses, Leonardo da Vinci. The narrower the range of interests which can be unified into the ' self,' the smaller the man.

The doctrine of the Holy Trinity, as Dr. Leonard Hodgson put it in his Croall Lectures on that doctrine, " asserts that all the unities of our earthly experience, from the unity of the hydrogen atom to the unity of a work of art, of the human self or of a human society, are imperfect instances of what unity truly is. We may find in them analogies of that true unity and learn from them something of what perfect unity must be. But perfect unity is to be found only in God, and it is through the revelation of God in Christ that we find the unity of God to be of such a kind as to cast light upon all our lesser unities . . . According to the revelation of Himself which God has given to us men in history there are three elements perfectly unified in the Divine life, and each of these elements is itself a Person . . . The act of faith required for acceptance of the doctrine of the Trinity is faith in this unification, faith that the Divine Unity is a dynamic unity, actively unifying in the one Divine life the lives of the three Divine Persons. It is a mystery, but not an irrational mystery. It is a mystery because on earth we have no experience of any unity which so perfectly unifies so wide and rich a diversity of content."

The practical consequences of this doctrine are that the Christian looks at the world with quite different eyes, even philosophically, from the non-Christian. Both have the same problem—to unify personality and experience. For both, it is still 'the Many and the One.' But they have different approaches, because different beliefs. One might even contend that every imperfect philosophy and every heresy demonstrates an attempt to achieve unity in the wrong way —by an attempt at reduction to a mathematical unity instead of by the dynamism of an organic unity. A pointer to such an analysis, which obviously cannot be made in detail here, is to see Epicureanism as focusing the unity on desire and making the will serve that end, while treating the reason as a 'rationalising' instrument; to see Stoicism as focusing the unity on the will, using desires and feelings as the will's material and the reason as the will's justification; and Scepticism as focusing the unity on the reason, subordinating to it both will and feelings.

But the true pattern of unity for men who are made in the image of the God who is the holy Trinity is that in which *all* the constituent parts are raised to their highest potentialities. The 'self' is the extreme development of all the 'selves,' not the rooting-out of all but one. It is not the individualisation which "views the simplification, the unification of man's interior life, as a gradually increasing abstraction" as Dom Theodore Wesseling has described this process in *Liturgy and Life*. "First it abstracts from the material world by a radical mortification; then it proceeds to abstract from fellow

creatures by throttling all affections, and this is called renounce-
ment; inside its own microcosm such a soul reduces first the
maintenance of the body to its minimum, then it tramples
the senses underfoot and tries to eliminate discursive reason
as if it were some obscurantist practice, till in the end—so it
hopes—pure intuition of the Absolute is the only thing left.
Thus the soul is emptied of itself and eagerly expects God to
come and live, like St. Sylvester, in an empty tomb . . . Such
a view is unreal to a degree and we should not be afraid of
calling it unorthodox in its ultimate analysis . . . Christ did
not pour His new wine into empty water-pots; He wanted
them to be filled with water ' to the brim ' and then He pro-
ceeded to transform the water into wine."

As life is short, we have not time here to realise all our
' selves.' But those we repress or suppress are not regarded
as inferior or evil, but as good things temporarily relinquished
for the love of God who has a particular work for us during
our little mortal day. The fullness of all is in heaven. That,
indeed, is the meaning of heaven and of the Beatific Vision—
the vision of the Holy Trinity.

On earth, " the man who is called to be a scholar must
curb his desire to engage in manifold practical activities. If
for a while he has to go and be a soldier, he must put aside
his civilian pursuits. If he is called to work in which marriage
is impossible, he must be continent with a good grace. But he
will only do any of these things with a good grace if he main-
tains a gracious attitude towards the selves he cannot satisfy.
This graciousness cannot be achieved except by the grace of
God. Our natural pride makes us disinclined to acknowledge
that we are finite beings who cannot foster all kinds of good,

it inclines us to justify our self-limitation by holding that we have chosen what is better and renounced what is worse . . . The achievement of a false unity in our own lives makes us incapable of taking a further step in graciousness and appreciating the contributions which others can make to human life just because they are different from our own. It may be that they are called to put in the centre selves which we have to put on one side." God himself entered the history of the world to re-make our human nature after the pattern of the divine Trinity and to offer heaven as the explanation of earth.

So the adoration of the Holy Trinity is also and incidentally an assertion of what humanity is and the challenge to paganism and pessimism in the certainty that " all manner of things shall be well." Beside it, other creeds look a little self-conscious and shrivelled.

Another way of understanding something of the doctrine is to stand imaginatively with the disciples as they were taught by Jesus. God the Father, they had understood from the beginning. Monotheism was part of their inheritance, as it is of ours. After the Resurrection, they could have no doubts that Jesus, too, was God. It was patent. And he had taught them continuously that He and his Father were one. Finally, with the coming of the Holy Spirit, they experienced another Divine Person—an advocate, a champion, strengthening, advising, defending them. In other words, they knew the Trinity, not as a dogma, but as an experience; not as a definition, but as recognisable Persons. So Christians have always experienced redemption—by the Father, through the Son, in the Spirit, and they require the defining only to express, as far as words can, the Truth for the sake of those whom, following their orders, they seek, as the apostles did, to bring to baptism in the Name of the Father and of the Son and of the holy Ghost.

(iii) " Amen "

The closing words of the Canon, *per omnia saecula saeculorum,* ' world without end,' are always said aloud (or, at High Mass, sung), so that the whole congregation assembled may respond with the ' Amen.' This Amen has been rightly called the most solemn in the whole liturgy of the Church. " It is the only word which requires the intervention of the congregation in the Great Prayer; it is essentially an act of faith in the mystery of the Great Action which has just been celebrated." All that has been said and done by the celebrant in the Canon is ratified by the people when they reply Amen.

The word itself, of course, is one of the few Hebrew words which have been taken unchanged into the worship of the Christian Church. That it was frequently on the lips of Christ —St. Matthew reports His use of it twenty-eight times—is sufficient to explain this. It comes from the Hebrew word meaning ' strengthen ' or ' confirm ' and it is the word—' so be it '—which unites him who prays with them who hear.

The Amen here at the end of the Canon is the primitive and important usage of it (the other ' Amens ' are later interpolations and are said, in any case, by the celebrant only) and Justin Martyr, in his account of the Eucharist, stresses that at the end of the Eucharistic Prayer " all the people that are present forthwith answer with acclamation ' Amen.' " So in the next century, St. Denis and in the next St. Ambrose and

St. Augustine extol the imposing exclamation "by all the people." "The great doxology" writes Fr. John Coventry in *The Breaking of Bread*, " is the final and triumphant elaboration of the theme of 'through Christ our Lord' which the Eucharistic Prayer introduces in its opening phrases and constantly resumes throughout. From the earliest times the whole people assembled finally answered the last pronouncement of the theme with their great act of assent, 'Amen.'"

It is well to remember, therefore, that this 'so be it' is different from every other assent to a prayer, in that this is a unique prayer and a unique action. This is the climax when we offer to God what is dearest to him and our own lives, at the same time setting before ourselves a way of life which will complete in us the mystery of the altar, in which we are all partakers. "Through Him and with Him and in Him . . . world without end, *Amen*."

AFTER THE CANON

(i) *The Lord's Prayer*

THE GREAT PRAYER has ended and the action of the Mass proceeds to the prayers and ceremonies of Communion. With these, as such, this little book is not concerned. Yet the immediate sequel—the Lord's Prayer, which unites all Christians, and the emphasis on unity, demonstrated in ritual, which precedes the Communion—are too relevant to be omitted. Moreover, they belong in time to the days of Gregory the Great and earlier, and were thus part of Augustine's first Mass at Canterbury in 597.

It was Gregory himself who decided that there was only one possible prayer to follow the great ' Amen.' No man-made intercession or thanksgiving could match that occasion. Nothing less than the prayer given us by Christ was adequate. So, after the ' Amen,' the Celebrant bids the people pray in these terms:

Instructed by Thy saving precepts and following Thy Divine instructions, we make bold to say: Our Father . . .

(praeceptis salutaribus moniti, et divina institutione formati, audemus dicere: Pater noster . . .)

This liturgical introduction to the Lord's Prayer is very ancient. More than a century before Gregory the Great's day, St. Jerome wrote that "Christ taught His apostles to presume, every day in the sacrifice of His Body, to say with faith: 'Our Father.'" And it is found, in some form, in all the rites. In the Greek liturgy of St. James, it runs: "Make us worthy, O Lord Who lovest mankind, with freedom and without condemnation, with a clean heart, with soul enlightened and with unashamed face and holy lips, to dare to call upon Thee, our Holy God and Father in Heaven and to say: 'Our Father . . .'" The exception was in the Ambrosian rite at Milan, where the Lord's Prayer was actually included in the Canon itself, after the *Per quem* and before the great Doxology.

Before Gregory the Great's time, the saying of the Our Father in the Roman rite came after the Kiss of Peace. This, too, constituted an additional reason for the change, for the Kiss was, above all, the demonstration of obedience to "Forgive us our trespasses as we forgive them that trespass against us."

The prayer, as it is understood at this point, recalls the theme of the meeting-place of heaven and earth, which has been announced in the *Supplices*. At the words "on earth as it is in Heaven," this used to be made explicit in a gesture. As the priest said *sicut in caelo et in terra* (the Latin form is necessary for the order) the Celebrant raised the Host on high once more at in *caelo* and replaced It on the altar at *in terra*. In some rites, also, the phrase was repeated by the people after each of the petitions which it qualifies—Hallowed be Thy Name: Thy Kingdom come: Thy will be done—

for it is not only the last to which it refers. We ask that God's Name may be blessed by men as it is by angels; that his Kingdom may come on earth as it already exists in heaven; and that on earth his will may be done as in heaven it is already perfectly accomplished.

And the Lord's Prayer takes on a new meaning, as placed here. Because it is, as Tertullian called it, a summary of the whole gospel, it is an affirmation of the moral law which binds those about to partake of the Body and blood of Christ. It is also in its first three phrases an epitome of the Canon itself. " Our Father Who art in Heaven, Hallowed be Thy Name on earth as it is in Heaven: Thy kingdom come on earth as it is in Heaven: Thy will be done on earth as it is in Heaven "—this is what we have been effecting. In the petition " Give us this day our daily bread " we look forward to the almost immediate reception of that bread. If the sentence, whenever said, has a Eucharistic significance, it becomes overwhelmingly apparent here. " Forgive us our trespasses as we forgive them that trespass against us " is the confession before communion; and " Lead us not into temptation but deliver us from evil " is a restatement of the prayer for the peace of God which has never been for long absent.

In our century this last petition has an added force when it is remembered that ' temptation ' had also once the meaning of torture. Perhaps only martyrs understand the full force of it—the agony lest they be tortured into apostasy despite the assurance: " You shall not be tempted more than you are able to bear." Seen thus, the final petition is really the consequence of thanksgiving—may our gratitude not be negatived by our weakness. It is not surprising, therefore, that Gregory

the Great elaborated the cry of the people " Deliver us from
evil" into the next prayer, which the Celebrant begins
immediately.

(ii) The Libera Nos

Deliver us, we beseech Thee, O Lord, from all evils past,
present and to come, and by the intercession of the blessed
and glorious Mary, ever Virgin Mother of God, and of Thy
holy Apostles Peter and Paul, and Andrew and of all the
Saints, mercifully grant peace in our days that through the
assistance of Thy mercy we may ever be free from sin and
secure from all disturbance, through Jesus Christ our Lord
Who liveth and reigneth with Thee in the unity of the
Holy Ghost, world without end, Amen.

Libera nos, quaesumus, Domine, ab omnibus malis,
praeteritis, praesentibus et futuris: et intercedente beata et
gloriosa semper Virgine Dei Genetrice Maria, cum beatis
Apostolis tuis Petro et Paulo, atque Andrea, et omnibus
Sanctis, da propitius pacem in diebus nostris: ut ope
misericordiae tuae adjuti, et a peccato simus semper liberi,
et ab omni pertrubatione securi.   Per eundem Dominum
nostrum Jesum Christum Filium Tuum Qui tecum vivit
et regnat in unitate Spiritus sancti Deus, per omnia saecula
saeculorum.   Amen.

The purpose of the *Libera* is sufficiently plain. The evil
from which we pray to be delivered is, in the first place, the
sin which would make us receive the body of Christ unworthily and, in the second, the kind of persecution which

might make it impossible for the Eucharist to be celebrated at all. The former is of the greater importance, since it is universal and continuing, whereas the latter, terrible though it is to its victims, is local and spasmodic. At this second petition we should pray above all for those who are persecuted to-day; at the first, we have no need to look beyond ourselves.

Immediately before Communion to-day comes the confession and absolution of sin; but here already the thought of the consequences of receiving the Host unworthily is implicit behind the prayer. " He that eateth and drinketh unworthily eateth and drinketh damnation to himself, not discerning the Lord's Body," wrote St. Paul in the earliest mention of the Eucharist in the New Testament; and this terrible warning has never long been absent from the thought of Christians. That it dictates the need for absolution needs no stressing; but it also has a particular bearing on the question of unity which non-Christians do not always understand.

A very common criticism is that the Church acts uncharitably and ' against the spirit of her Master ' in denying communion to those ' of good will ' who are not ' practising Christians '—and even to those who are baptised Christians but who do not accept the ' Lord's Supper ' as anything but a memorial meal. But what else, in charity to *them*, dare the Church do? For their separation from the Church is caused precisely by the fact that they do *not* perceive the Lord's body. They eat the ' bread ' to revive a memory or take part in a conventional observance which, to them, means something different from what the Church means. How can the Church, caring for them even though they are outside it, allow them so to court damnation? And it is surely a pertinent question whether, if they knew the Faith as it is enshrined in the Great Prayer, they would want to. Is it not only because their idea of 'christianity' is something altogether different from the faith which St. Augustine brought to England that the difficulty arises?

There is one place in the *Libera* where our thoughts inevitably turn to this tragic difference between then and now —the mention of St. Andrew. This is the only time in which his name appears in such a context in the entire Liturgy and the historical reason takes us back to the end of the sixth century, and the missionary zeal of Gregory the Great.

The story of Gregory in the slave-market at Rome, seeing the fair-haired boys from the North, designating them 'not Angles but angels' and promising the Alleluia should be sung in the land of King Aella, needs no retelling. But the background of Gregory at this time is less well-known. As the young Prefect of Rome, this brilliant and wealthy patrician lived in his ancestral palace on the Caelian Hill. After relinquishing his office, he became a Benedictine monk and turned that palace into a monastery. He dedicated it to St. Andrew, the patron saint of missionary endeavour (because he had been the first to find Jesus and had brought his brother Peter to Him). First as a monk, later as Prior, Gregory's friend Augustine was a member of the monastery of St. Andrew; and it was to him that Gregory, when he became Pope, entrusted the task of evangelising England with the aid of forty of the St. Andrew's monks.

Leaving the security of the monastery for the perils of the unknown north, they were, half-way to England, seized " with a sudden fear, and began to think of returning home rather than to proceed to a barbarous, fierce, unbelieving nation to whose very language they were strangers." Augustine so far gave way to their fears as to return to lay the case before Gregory, who replied in the famous letter: "Gregory, the servant of the servants of God, to the servants of our Lord: Forasmuch as it had been better not to begin a good work than to think of desisting from that which is begun, it behoves you, my beloved sons, to fulfil the good work which, by the help of our Lord, you have undertaken." And, mastering their fears, the monks of St. Andrew's went on to win England for the Cross.

It is surely legitimate to suppose that as St. Augustine said the *Libera* at the first Mass at Canterbury, the name of St. Andrew, which Gregory had inserted as a personal devotion to the patron he had chosen for the monastery that was their home, must have had a significance which it is impossible for us now to estimate. But at least we may pray that, with Augustine's task still uncompleted and Gregory's dream still unrealised, we may spare no efforts, St. Andrew aiding us, "till we all come in the unity of the Faith and of the knowledge of the Son of God unto a perfect man, unto the measure of the stature of the fullness of Christ: that we henceforth be no more children, tossed to and fro and carried about with every wind of doctrine, by the sleight of men and cunning craftiness, whereby they lie in wait to deceive."

On one day and one day only is the *Libera* said aloud—in the Mass of the Presanctified on Good Friday. 'The Mass of the Presanctified' is the name given to the priest's communion from the Host which was consecrated on Maundy Thursday, for on Good Friday itself no Consecration can be effected.

The whole of the Canon is therefore omitted and the first prayer (of those we have been considering) said is the *Our Father*, followed by the *Libera*. During the saying of this prayer, the celebrant breaks the Host into three parts, of which the smallest—the Particle—is dropped into the Chalice. This happens in every Mass and is part of the ritual we are about to consider. But on Good Friday, the difference is that the chalice contains *wine only*. It is not the Blood, for there has been no consecration. This, which is known as the *commixtio*, the mingling, is a primitive custom and suggests that " by contact with the Lord's Body the wine was sanctified and thus in a certain sense, took the place of the species which was not consecrated on that day."

There is another reason for the importance given to the *Libera* on Good Friday. From about the year 800 in the West and three hundred years earlier in the East, this part of the Mass was taken to represent the Passion, the ' breaking ' of Christ's body, a symbolism which ended with the mingling which represented the Resurrection. Just before the *commixtio*, this idea is made explicit. With the Particle, the celebrant makes a three-fold sign of the Cross over the Chalice—recalling the three days of Christ's entombment—saying as he does so: " The peace of the Lord be always with you "—Pax Domini sit semper vobiscum—which was Jesus's own Easter greeting. At this point, in primitive times, the entire congregation exchanged the Kiss of Peace.

The symbolism goes deeper still. At High Mass (which, of course, is the norm of Mass: Low Mass, said by the celebrant alone without either deacon or sub-deacon, is a later and ' utilitarian ' development) the sub-deacon has stood

throughout the Canon at the bottom of the steps leading up
to the altar. Round his shoulders is the ' humeral veil,' under
which he holds the paten on which the Host will lie. At the
end of the Lord's Prayer, he comes up to the altar and the
paten is handed to the celebrant. During the Libera, at the
invocation of the saints, the celebrant crosses himself with the
paten and then kisses it after the words " grant peace in our
days." He puts the Host on it; then taking it up, he breaks
it in half before saying " through Jesus Christ thy Son our
Lord." Replacing the half which he holds in his right hand
on the paten, he then from the part which remains in his left
hand breaks off the particle as he says " Who liveth and reigneth
with thee in the unity of the Holy Ghost."

Behind these actions lie a tremendous assertion of unity
which can be understood only by knowing the history of
them. Probably from the second century, certainly from the
fifth, it was the custom for the Pope (or, if not in Rome, the
bishop) to break off portions from his Host and send them,
by the hands of acolytes or sub-deacons, to every priest
celebrating the Eucharist in churches nearby. Each priest put
this *fermentum*, ' leaven ' as it was called, with reference to
Christ's parable of the leaven, into his own chalice. Thus
was demonstrated that there was, in reality, only one Mass
in *place*.

There was another ceremony, almost identical with it,
showing that there was only one Mass in *time*. At each Mass
everywhere, a particle of the Host would be broken off and
reserved until the next day. This, known as the *sancta*, the
sacred piece, was added to the Chalice of the next day's Mass.
Thus what the sub-deacon with the humeral veil was once

holding was not, as it is to-day, an empty paten, but a paten on which was resting the consecrated Body (which explains the name, humeral veil). When, during the *Our Father*, he brought it to the altar, it was that the celebrant might mingle it with the newly-consecrated Chalice.

Thus was proclaimed in ritual that there is, in reality, only one Mass in the whole world, which is the Last Supper; that in the Eucharist, time and place disappear in the eternal moment when earth and heaven meet. And this unity, proclaimed at this ritual point of ' Easter,' is given one further emphasis. The Sacramental Body, broken, has by the *commixtio* been made one again; the Mystical Body, too, must be seen as one. And by the Kiss of Peace, beginning from the celebrant and extended, though not now to the congregation, to everyone in the sanctuary down to the youngest acolyte, this is effected.

The actual prayer which the celebrant to-day says before giving the kiss of peace to the deacon is one which, rightly, has been adopted as the general prayer for unity. With it, fitly, this little commentary (whose only purpose is to foster understanding which may bring that Unity nearer) may close:

O Lord Jesu Christ, Who saidst to Thine Apostles: Peace I leave with you; My peace I give unto you: regard not my sins, but the faith of Thy Church and vouchsafe to grant her peace and unity according to Thy will: Who livest and reignest God, throughout all ages, world without end. Amen.

London, Maundy Thursday, 1954